VERGIL'S AENEID

Selections from Books 1, 2, 4, 6, 10, and 12

Teacher's Guide

Barbara Weiden Boyd

Bolchazy-Carducci Publishers, Inc.
Wauconda, Illinois

General Editor
Laurie Haight Keenan

Contributing Editor
James Chochola

Cover Design & Typography
Adam Phillip Velez

Cover Illustration
"Into the Darkened City"
by Thom Kapheim

Vergil's *Aeneid:* **Selections from Books 1, 2, 4, 6, 10, and 12**
Teacher's Guide

© **copyright 2002 Bolchazy-Carducci Publishers, Inc.**
All rights reserved.

Bolchazy-Carducci Publishers, Inc.
1000 Brown Street
Wauconda, IL 60084 USA
www.bolchazy.com

Printed in the United States of America
2006
by Publisher's Graphics

ISBN-13: 978-0-86516-481-9
ISBN-10: 0-86516-481-9

CONTENTS

INTRODUCTION

The contents of this supplementary volume are meant to serve as aids to teachers and to students working independently on the Aeneid. The literal translation is just that: I have attempted to reflect in English as much as possible the syntax and structure of Vergil's Latin, and have studiously attempted not to obscure the difficulty of some of Vergil's language. I have maintained the tenses of the verbs as they appear in Latin, although this may sound ungainly to the reader not long familiar with this flexible feature of literary Latin. When I have found it necessary to supplement the translation with occasional words or phrases to clarify the sense of a given passage, I have put the supplementary material in square brackets; parentheses are used only where they appear in the printed Latin text as well.

The list of questions for discussion and analysis is meant to help teachers and readers new to the passages covered in the companion volume by encouraging thoughtfulness about the readings and provoking discussion. I rarely consider one and only one answer to be the "right" one; rather, I encourage all my readers to take these questions as a starting-point for open-ended and, I hope, productive discussion. These questions are not by any means the only ones that can be asked about the passages considered here, and I encourage my readers to develop questions of their own to pose. The texts under consideration ably demonstrate the inherent wealth of Vergil's creativity, capable of stirring anew emotion and thoughtfulness in each subsequent generation. I am delighted to have the opportunity to make this wealth more accessible to my readers.

This Teacher's Guide also includes a "clean" copy of the Latin text based on the R. A. B. Mynors' 1969 edition of the Oxford Classical Text, free of the special formatting used in the textbook (i.e., mixed typefaces and macrons). Teachers are encouraged to incorporate this text into classwork and tests so that students will be prepared for the appearance of the text on the actual AP* exam, and of other Latin texts they may encounter in college courses or elsewhere. As always, I encourage teachers to remind students that macrons were not written in ancient texts, but are a modern linguistic and pedagogical device. The "clean" text is meant to help students and teachers alike experience Vergil's poem with as little editorial intrusion as possible.

BARBARA WEIDEN BOYD
Bowdoin College

*AP is a registered trademark of the College Entrance Examination Board, which was not involved in the production of, and does not endorse, this product.

A LITERAL TRANSLATION OF VERGIL'S *AENEID*
SELECTIONS FROM BOOKS 1, 2, 4, 6, 10, & 12

Note: Words and phrases in square brackets are generally supplements to (or, in a very few cases, subtractions from) the Latin text, intended in all cases to clarify for the reader Vergil's meaning. Parentheses are used only where they appear in the Latin text (OCT), or where there would otherwise be double brackets.

AENEID 1.1–519

1.1–33

I sing of arms and of the man who first [as] an exile from the shores of Troy, because of fate, came to Italy and the Lavinian shores; that man [having been] tossed about a great deal both on land and at sea by the power of the gods, on account of the unforgetting wrath of cruel Juno, and having endured much also in war, until he could found a city and bring [his] gods into Latium; whence [i.e., from this origin] [came] the Latin people and the Alban fathers and the walls of lofty Rome. Muse, recall to me the reasons: with what divine power having been wounded [i.e., as the result of harm done to what divine power] or grieving at what did the queen of the gods compel a man outstanding in devotion [i.e., to gods, home, and family] to endure so many misfortunes, confront so many struggles? Do the heavenly spirits possess wrath[s] of such magnitude?

There was an ancient city (Tyrian settlers possessed it), Carthage, far opposite Italy and the mouth[s] of the Tiber, rich in resources and most fierce in the pursuits of war, which alone Juno is said to have cherished more than all [other] lands, preferred even to Samos [lit., Samos being held in second place]. Here [were] her weapons, here was [her] chariot; the queen even now intends and nurtures this [place] to be the kingdom [i.e., ruling power] for [its] peoples, if the fates should permit [this] in any way. But indeed she had heard that offspring which would one day overturn the Tyrian citadel[s] was being produced from Trojan blood; from this [i.e., offspring *or* event] would come a people ruling broadly and proud in war for the destruction of

Libya; [and had heard that] the Fates were unrolling [the destiny of Carthage] thus. The Saturnian, fearing this and mindful of the old war, because she had first [or formerly] waged [war] at Troy on behalf of her beloved Argives— and not even yet had the causes of her wrath[s] and her cruel sorrows fallen from [her] mind; buried in [her] deep mind [i.e., buried deep in her mind] remains the judgment of Paris and the insult to her rejected beauty and the hated people and the honors of [i.e., given to] stolen Ganymede [or the stolen honors of Ganymede]: inflamed on account of these things, she was keeping far off from Latium the Trojans, tossed about upon the entire sea, the remnants of [i.e., left by] the Greeks and cruel Achilles, and they were wandering for many years, driven by the fates around all the seas. [Of] so great a struggle was it to found the Roman people.

1.34–49

Scarcely out of sight of the Sicilian land the men happily [lit., the happy men] were setting sail onto the deep [sea] and were plowing the foam of the salt [sea] with their bronze [i.e., their bronze-tipped prows], when Juno, preserving the everlasting wound under her breast [or deep in her heart,] [said] these things with [i.e., to] herself: "Am I, having been defeated, to cease from [my] undertaking, and to not be able to turn away from Italy the king of the Teucrians [i.e., Trojans]? Of course, I am prevented by the fates. Was Pallas [Minerva] able to burn up the fleet of the Argives and to drown the men themselves in the sea on account of the insult and madness of one man, Ajax son of Oileus? She herself, having hurled the swift fire of Jupiter from the clouds, both scattered the ships and overturned the sea with the winds, and him she snatched up in a whirlwind [as he was] breathing out flames from his transfixed breast, and she impaled [him] on a sharp crag. But I, who proceed as queen of the gods and both sister and wife of Jupiter, have been waging war [lit., do wage war] with a single people for so many years [now]. And who will worship [lit., worships] the divinity of Juno hereafter or, [as] a suppliant, will place an offering on [her] altars?"

1.50–80

Pondering such things with [or to] herself in her inflamed heart, the goddess comes to the the country of the clouds, a place teeming with the raging south winds, Aeolia. Here in his vast cave king Aeolus controls with authority the struggling winds and howling storms and reins [them] in with the restraints of [his] prison [lit., with chains and with prison]. Chafing, they rumble around the barriers [i.e., the prison containing them] with a great roar of the mountain; Aeolus sits on his lofty citadel holding his scepter[s], and he both soothes [their] spirits and calms [their] wrath[s]. Were he not to do

[this], the swift [winds] would surely carry off with themselves the seas and lands and the deep heaven, and would sweep [them] through the air. But fearing this, the all-powerful father hid [them] in dark caves, and set above [them] a mass and lofty mountains [i.e., a mass of lofty mountains], and gave them a [i.e., the sort of] king who would know both how to restrain [them] by means of a clear agreement and how, [when] ordered, to give loose reins [i.e, slacken his hold on the reins.] To him then Juno [as] suppliant employed these words:

"Aeolus (since the father of gods and king of men granted to you [the ability] to soothe the waves and to raise [them] with the wind), a people hostile to me sails the Tyrrhenian sea, carrying Troy and [its *or* their] conquered household gods into Italy. Strike violence into the winds and overwhelm the submerged ships [i.e., overwhelm and submerge the ships], or drive [the Trojans] in different directions and scatter their bodies on the sea. There are [in my possession] twice seven nymphs of outstanding physical beauty, of whom Deiopea, who is most beautiful in form [*or* There are in my possession twice seven Nymphs of outstanding beauty; she who is the the most beautiful of these in form, Deiopea], I shall join [to you] in stable marriage and shall declare your own, so that she may live [lit., carry through] all her years with you in return for such merits [i.e., in return for this favor] and so that she may make you a father of fair offspring."

Aeolus [spoke] these words in response: "[It is] your task, queen, to search out what you wish; for me it is right to undertake what has been ordered [lit., the ordered things]. Whatever [of] kingdom this is you win over for me, you unite [to me] the scepter[s] [i.e., of power] and Jupiter, you grant [to me] to recline at the feasts of the gods and you make [me] the one ruling [i.e., the ruler of] clouds and storms."

1.81–123

When these [words had been] said, he struck the hollow mountain against its side with [his] spear reversed [*or* reversed spear]; and the winds rush forth, just as [when] a battle line [has been] drawn up [lit., a battle-line having been drawn up], where a gateway [is] given, and they blow through the lands in a whirlwind [*or* in the manner of a whirlwind]. [Now] they brooded over the sea, and the East wind and South wind together, and the Southwest wind thick with squalls, heave up the whole [sea] from [its] deep foundations, and roll huge waves toward the shores. The shouting of men and the grating of the ropes follow[s]; suddenly the clouds snatch both the sky and day [i.e., daylight] out of the eyes [i.e., sight] of the Teucrians [i.e., Trojans]; black night broods over the sea; and the poles thundered and the upper air flashes with frequent [bursts of] fires, and everything threatens the men with imminent death [lit., all things aim imminent death at the men].

Suddenly Aeneas' limbs are loosened with cold [i.e., fear]; he groans, and out-stretching to the stars his two hands he says such things with [his] voice: "O three and four times fortunate, [those] to whom it befell to encounter [death] before the faces of [their] fathers beneath the lofty walls of Troy! O son of Tydeus, strongest of the people of the Danaans! Could I not have fallen on the Trojan plains and poured forth this soul at [i.e., by means of] your right hand, where fierce Hector lies because of the spear of the grandson of Aeacus [i.e., Achilles], where huge Sarpedon [lies], where the river Simois rolls beneath [its] waves so many snatched shields of men, and [their] helmets and brave bodies?"

As he was [lit., to him] uttering such things, a roaring gust from the North wind strikes the sail head-on, and raises the waves to the stars. The oars are broken, then the prow turns away and offers the side [of the ship] to the waves, [and] a towering mountain of water pursues in a mass. These men [i.e., some men] hang on the top of a wave; a gaping wave reveals the earth among the waves for these [i.e., other men], [and] the surge rages in the [or with] sand[s]. The South wind whirls three [ships] [that have been] snatched up onto the lurking rocks (the rocks in the middle of the waves which the Italians call "Altars," a huge ridge on the surface of the sea), the East wind drives three [ships] from the deep onto the shallows and reefs, wretched to see, and dashes [them] on the shoals and encircles them with a mound of sand. One [i.e., of the ships], which was carrying the Lycians and trusty Orontes, the huge sea from high above beats against the prow before the eyes of him himself [i.e., before Aeneas' eyes]; and the pilot is struck out [of the ship] face-first and rolls headlong, but the wave, driving that [ship] around three times, whirls it in the same place, and the swift whirlpool swallows [it] up in the sea. Men appear here and there [lit., scattered] swimming in the vast whirlpool, the weapons of men and planks [i.e., of the ship] and Trojan treasure [scattered] through the waves. Now the storm has overcome the strong ship of Ilioneus, now [that] of brave Achates, and [the ship] on which Abas [was] carried, and [that] on which aged Aletes [was carried]; the seams of the sides having been loosened [i.e., since the seams of the ships' sides had become loose], they all [i.e., all the ships] take on hostile water and gape with cracks.

1.124–56

Meanwhile, Neptune, gravely disturbed, sensed that the sea was being confused with a great rumbling and that a storm [had been] sent forth and that the still waters [had been] poured back from [or to] the depths of the sea, and looking out over the deep sea he raised [his] peaceful head from the top of the water. He sees the fleet of Aeneas scattered on the entire sea, [and] the Trojans overwhelmed by waves and by the downfall of heaven; nor did the tricks and wrath of Juno escape the notice of [her] brother. He calls the East and West winds to himself, [and] thereupon speaks such things: "Has so great a confidence in your origin taken hold of you? Do you dare now, winds, to stir up heaven and earth without my divine power and to raise such great masses [i.e., of confusion]? [You] whom I—but it is better to compose the waves [that have been] disturbed. Afterwards you will atone for your crimes to me with a different [lit., not similar] punishment. Speed [your] flight and say these things to your king: not to him [has been] given by lot the rule of the sea and the cruel trident, but to me. He possesses huge rocks, your home[s], East wind; let Aeolus toss himself about in that hall and rule, after the winds have been shut in their prison [lit., with the prison of the winds having been shut]."

Thus he speaks, and more swiftly than speech [lit., than a word] he calms the swollen seas and puts the assembled clouds to flight and brings back the sun. Together Cymothoe and Triton, pushing, dislodge the ships from the sharp rock; he himself [i.e., Neptune] raises [them] with [his] trident and reveals the huge sandbars and calms the sea and glides along the top of the waves with swift wheels. And just as when, as often [i.e., as often happens], a riot has begun in a great populace, and the common crowd rages in spirit[s] [or with anger] and now torches and rocks fly, [and] madness supplies weapons; then, if by chance they catch sight [lit., have caught sight] of any man solemn in devotion and service[s], they fall silent and stand with [their] ears pricked up [lit., their ears having been raised]; he rules their minds with [his] words and soothes [their] hearts: thus subsided the entire uproar of the sea, after the father, looking out on the seas and conveyed in the open sky, guides [his] horses and gives rein, flying along, to [his] obedient chariot.

1.157–207

Exhausted, the followers of Aeneas struggle to seek the shores which [are] closest on [their] course [or with haste], and are turned [i.e, turn] to the coasts of Libya. There is a place in a long recess: an island creates a port with the projection of [its] sides, by [means of] which every wave from the deep is broken, and splits itself into recessed bays. From this side and from that, vast crags and twin cliffs [extending] into the sky tower, beneath the summit of which the safe waters are silent far and wide; then from above [there is] a stage-set with quivering woods, and a black grove threatens with bristling shade. Under the opposite face [there is] a cave [made out] of suspended stone; within [there are] sweet waters and seats [made out] of the living rock, the home of the nymphs. Here no chains hold exhausted ships, no anchor binds [them] with its hooked bite. Aeneas enters this place with seven ships gathered from the entire number [i.e., of ships], and, disembarking, the Trojans take possession of the longed-for sand with a great love for land, and set [their] bodies [lit., limbs] dripping with salt [i.e., salt-water] on the shore.

And first of all, Achates struck a spark from a flint, and took up the fire with leaves, and gave around [i.e., scattered] dry nourishment[s] [i.e., kindling], and caught the flame in the tinder. Then the men, exhausted from the events [i.e., the storm], prepare the grain [lit., Ceres] spoiled by the waters and the tools for preparing the grain, and they prepare to roast the recovered grain[s] with flames and to grind [it] with stone.

Meanwhile, Aeneas climbs the cliff, and seeks all the view far and wide on the sea, if [i.e., in the hope that] he may see any [sign of] Antheus tossed by the wind, and the Phrygian biremes, or Capys, or the weapons of Caicus on the high prow[s]. He sees no ship in sight, [but] three stags wandering on the shore; entire herds follow them from the rear and the long line grazes through [the length of] the valleys. He took a stand here and snatched with [his] hand the bow and swift arrows, the weapons which loyal Achates was carrying, and first lays low the leaders [of the herd] themselves bearing heads lofty with tree-like antlers, then he confuses the herd and the entire crowd, driving [them] with [his] weapons among the leafy groves. Nor does he stop before, [as] victor, he lays low seven huge bodies on the ground and matches their number with [that of] the ships. From here, he seeks the port, and divides [the spoils] among all [his] companions. He distributes the wine which the good hero Acestes had then [i.e., when still back at Sicily] loaded in jars on the Sicilian shore and had given them as they were departing [lit., to the departing ones], and he soothes [their] grieving hearts with words:

"O companions (for neither are we ignorant of troubles before), o men having suffered more severe things, the god will give a limit to these [things], too. You have both approached the Scyllaean rage and the deeply resounding cliffs, and you [have] experienced the Cyclopian rocks. Call back your spirits and let go of sorrowful fear; perhaps at some time [in the future] it will be pleasing to remember even these things. We head into Latium, where the fates show [us] quiet home[s], through varied misfortunes, through so many dangers of things. There it is right for the kingdom of Troy to rise again. Endure, and save yourselves for favorable conditions."

1.207–22

He says such things with [his] voice, and [though] sick with huge cares he feigns hope on [his] face, [and] presses his grief deep in his heart. They gird themselves for booty and [their] feasts about to be [i.e., future feasts]; they tear the hides from the ribs and lay bare the innards; some cut [the meat] into pieces, and fasten them, [still] quivering, on the spits, [while] others place bronze [vessels] on the shore and tend the flames. Then they restore [their] strength[s] with food, and reclining [lit., extended] through the grass, they are filled of [i.e, with] old Bacchus and rich venison. After [their] hunger [had been] taken away by the feasts and the tables [had been] removed, they seek again their lost companions through lengthy conversation, doubtful between hope and fear whether they should believe that [they] [i.e., the companions] are alive, or whether [they should believe that] they are experiencing their final fate[s] and, having been called, no longer hear. Especially loyal Aeneas now [laments the misfortune] of spirited Orontes, now he laments the misfortune of Amycus, and the cruel fates of Lycus with [i.e., to] himself, and brave Gyas, and brave Cloanthus.

1.223–96

And now there was an end [i.e., of eating and talking], when Jupiter, looking down from lofty heaven onto the sea winged with sails and the lands lying [i.e., outstretched] and the coastlines and the broad [i.e., spread far and wide] peoples, thus took a stand on the summit of heaven and fixed [his] eyes on the kingdoms of Libya. And Venus, rather sad, and her shining eyes filled with tears [lit., filled with tears in respect to her shining eyes], addressed that one, pondering such cares in [his] heart: "O you who rule the affairs of both mortals and gods with eternal authority and who terrify with lightning, what so great [thing was] my Aeneas [able] to commit against you, what were the Trojans able [to commit against you], to whom, having suffered so many deaths, the entire globe of earth is shut on account of Italy? Surely [you] promised that from this origin, as the years roll by, at some time in the future, there would be Romans, from this origin there would be leaders, from the restored bloodline of Teucer, who [would hold] the sea [and] would hold all the lands under [their] control; what intention, father, turns you [i.e., away from this promise]? I used indeed to [try to] find consolation in this [i.e., the promise] for the fall of Troy and the sad ruins, balancing fates opposing fates; now, the same (mis)chance pursues [the] men driven by so many misfortunes. What limit for [their] struggles do you give, great king? Having escaped from the middle [i.e., midst] of the Achaeans, Antenor was able, safe[ly], to enter the Illyrian gulfs and the deepest kingdoms of the Liburnians, and to pass beyond the source of the Timavus, whence through nine mouths [the river] goes with the vast rumbling of a mountain, [as goes] a sea having burst forth, and overwhelms the plowed fields with [its] resounding flood. Here nevertheless that man placed the city of Patavium and the seats [i.e., homes] of the Trojans, and he gave a name to the people and he fastened Trojan arms [i.e., to the temple at which he had dedicated them as a sign of gratitude for divine favor]; now, composed in calm quiet, he rests; [but] we, your offspring, to whom you promise the citadel of heaven, are betrayed, our ships (unspeakable!) having been lost on account of the wrath of one, and are separated far from the Italian shores. [Is] this the reward for loyalty? Thus do [i.e., is this how] you restore us into the scepters [i.e., power]?"

Smiling at that one with the face with which he calms the sky and storms, the begetter of men and of gods touched [i.e., with a kiss] the lips of [his] daughter, [and] thereafter says such things: "Spare [your] fear [i.e., don't fear], Cytherea, the fates of your people remain unshaken for you; you will see the city and the promised walls of Lavinium, and will bear aloft to the stars of heaven great-spirited Aeneas; and [my] opinion does not change me. This one (for I shall speak, since this care gnaws at you, and unrolling the secrets of the fates farther [i.e., from a distance] I shall stir [them] up) will wage a great war for you in Italy and will crush fierce peoples and will establish customs and walls for [his] men, until a third summer will have seen [him] ruling in Latium and three winters [i.e., periods during which winter quarters are set up] will have passed, the Rutulians having been subdued. But the boy Ascanius, to whom the cognomen Iulus is now given (he was Ilus, while the Ilian state stood in power), will fill out thirty great cycles [of years] in power as the months roll by [lit., with the months rolling], and will transfer [his] rule from the seat of Lavinium, and will fortify Alba Longa with much strength. Here in turn it will be ruled [i.e., there will be the seat of rule] three times a hundred whole years under the Hectorean people [i.e., of Hector], until the priestess queen Ilia, pregnant by Mars, will give in birth twin offspring. Thence Romulus, happy in [i.e., because of] the tawny pelt of the she-wolf nurse, will inherit [the] people and will found the Martian walls [i.e., of Mars] and will call [the people] Romans from his own name. For these people I set neither limits of things nor times; I have given [them] authority without limit. Indeed, even harsh Juno, who now wearies sea and earth and heaven with fear, will recall her plans into [i.e., for] the better, and with me will cherish the Romans, the masters of things [i.e., of all things *or* of the world] and the toga-clad people. It [has] thus pleased [the fates]. A season will come, the periods of years gliding by, when the house of Assaracus will subject in slavery Phthia and famed Mycenae, and will rule over conquered Argos. Of fair origin will be born Trojan Caesar, who will limit [his] authority with Ocean, [his] fame with the stars, Julius [Caesar], a name derived from great Iulus. Free of care, you will at some time [in the future] receive him in heaven, laden with the spoils of the East; he too will be called upon with prayers. Then, wars having been set aside, harsh ages will become mild; white-haired Fides and Vesta, Quirinus [i.e., Romulus] with his brother Remus will give [i.e., establish] laws; the awful gates of [the god of] war [i.e., Janus] will be shut with iron and close-fitting fastenings; unholy Furor, sitting within atop cruel weapons and bound with one hundred brazen knots behind [his] back [i.e., with his hands tied behind his back] will rage horrible [i.e., horribly] with his bloody mouth."

1.297–304

He says these things and sends down from on high the [son] born of Maia [i.e., Mercury], so that the lands and so that [the] new citadels of

Carthage may lie open for hospitality for the Trojans, lest Dido, unaware of [her *or* their] fate, might keep [them] from [her] territories. He flies through the great air with the oarage of wings, and swift[ly] stood on the shores of Libya. And now he makes [i.e., gives] the commands, and the Phoenicians set aside [their] fierce hearts since the god [so] wills [it] [lit., the god willing]. The queen especially takes up a calm attitude and kindly intent toward the Trojans.

1.305–71

But devoted Aeneas, turning over very many things [i.e., thoughts] through the night, as soon as kindly [day]light was given, resolved to go out and to investigate the new places, to inquire what shores he had reached by means of the wind, who possesses them, humans or wild beasts (for he sees [that the territories are] wild), and to report the things discovered [by him] to his companions. He conceals the fleet, shut in all around by trees and bristling shadows, in the hollow of groves beneath a hollowed-out crag. He himself, accompanied by Achates alone, proceeds, brandishing in [his] hand two spear-shafts with [their] broad iron [i.e., blade]. To whom [i.e., to him] [his] mother brought herself face-to-face in the middle of the forest, bearing the face and garb of a maiden, and a Spartan maiden's weapons, or [of a maiden] such as the Thracian Harpalyce, [who] tires her horses and surpasses the swift Hebrus in flight. For the huntress had suspended from her shoulder in the [usual] manner an easily-handled bow, and had given her hair to the winds to scatter, bare at the knee and having gathered [lit., having been gathered with respect to] the flowing folds [of her gown] in a knot. And she spoke first: "Hello, young men! Show me if you have seen any one of [my] sisters wandering here by chance, [her dress] girded, with a quiver and the covering of a spotted lynx, or pressing the chase of a frothing boar with a shout."

So [spoke] Venus, and the son of Venus spoke thus in return: "None of your sisters [has been] heard or seen by me, o—[but] how should I call [i.e., name] you, maiden? For you have [lit., to you there is] a face not [lit., hardly] mortal, nor does [your] voice sound [of a] human. O, goddess surely (a sister of Phoebus? or one of the blood [i.e., family] of the nymphs?), may you, whoever [you are], be propitious, and may you relieve our struggle and may you explain, at last, under what sky [and] on which shores of earth we are tossed; we wander ignorant of both people and places, driven to this place by wind and vast waves. Many a sacrificial victim will fall for you before [your] altars by my [lit., our] right hand."

Then Venus [spoke]: "Not at all [lit., hardly] to be sure do I deem myself worthy of such honor; it is the custom for Tyrian maidens to carry the quiver and to bind [their] shins high up with the purple [hunting-]boot. You see the Punic kingdoms, the Tyrians and the city of Agenor; but the territories [are] Libyan, a people intractable in war. Having departed from the Tyrian city, fleeing [her] brother, Dido rules [this] kingdom. Long is the [story of her] injustice [i.e., the injustice done to her], long [are] the twists and turns [i.e., of the story]; but I shall follow the highest points of things [i.e., of the story]. To this woman Sychaeus was husband, wealthiest of the Phoenicians in gold, and cherished by the great love of [his] unfortunate [wife], to whom [her] father had given her untouched and [to whom he] had joined [i.e., married] [her] by means of the first auspices [i.e., the auspices for a first marriage]. But [her] brother Pygmalion held the rule of Tyre, more monstrous in crime before [i.e., than] all others. Between whom [i.e., between the two men] came madness in [their] midst. That one [Pygmalion], disloyal and blinded by the love of gold, surreptitiously overcomes before the altars the unsuspecting Sychaeus with iron [i.e., a sword], heedless of the loves of his sister; and for a long time he hid the deed, and pretending much, the evil one deceived the [love-]sick lover with empty hope. But the image [i.e., likeness] itself of the unburied husband came in [her] dream[s], lifting up his face[s] pale in strange ways; it [i.e., the image] laid bare the cruel altars and the breast[s] pierced by the iron, and disclosed the entire hidden crime of the house. Then it [i.e., the image] persuades [her] to hasten flight and to depart from the country, and [as] an aid for the journey, reveals the old treasures [buried] in the ground [*or* from the ground], an unknown weight of silver and gold. Moved by these [revelations], Dido prepared her comrades for flight [lit., was preparing flight and comrades]. [Those] to whom there was [i.e., who had] either a cruel hatred of the tyrant or sharp fear gather together. The ships, which by chance [had been] prepared, they seize and load with gold. The riches of greedy Pygmalion are carried on [*or* by] the sea; the leader of the deed [is] a woman. They arrived at the place[s] where now you will see huge walls and the rising citadel of new Carthage, and purchased as much ground—[called] Byrsa from the name of the deed—as they were able to surround with a bull's hide.

"But you—who, at last, [are you]? Or from what shores have you come? Or to where do you hold course [i.e., where are you headed]?" To her asking [these things], he, sighing, and drawing [his] voice [i.e., words] from his deep heart [responded] with such [words]:

1.372–417

"O goddess, if I were to proceed retracing from the first beginning [i.e., of the story] and there were spare time to hear the records of our struggles, sooner will the evening star settle the day, [the doors of] Olympus having been shut. From ancient Troy—if perchance the name of Troy has gone through your ears—a storm, by means of its own fate, drove us, carried through various seas, to the Libyan shores. I am faithful Aeneas, by reputation known above the skies, who carry with me by means of the fleet the household gods snatched from the enemy. I seek [our] homeland Italy [*or* I seek Italy to be our homeland], and the origin from highest Jupiter. With twice ten ships I embarked on the Phrygian sea [i.e., the sea off the coast of Troy], following the fates given [to me and] with the goddess my mother showing the way. Scarcely do seven [i.e., ships] survive, torn by the waves and East wind. Unknown [or unknowing] [and] in need, I myself wander through the wastes of Libya, driven from Europe and Asia." Venus, not allowing him to lament more [lit., him lamenting more things/words], interrupted [him] thus in the middle of [his] grief:

"Whoever you are, not at all, I believe, hateful to the heavenly ones [i.e., the gods], you consume [lit., pluck] life-giving breezes, you who have arrived at the Tyrian city [or since you have arrived at the Tyrian city]. Just proceed, and from here betake yourself to the threshold[s] of the queen. For I announce that [your] allies [are] restored to you, and [your] fleet [has been] carried back and driven by the changed North winds into safety [lit., into a safe (place)], unless [my] false [i.e., deceptive] parents taught [me] augury in vain. See twice ten swans rejoicing in a line, which the bird of Jupiter, having fallen from the heavenly region, was throwing into confusion in the open sky: now they seem either to take earth [i.e., alight] in a long line, or to look down on the earth already taken [i.e., alighted upon] [by the other birds in the flock]. Just as they, restored, with whirring wings play, and encircle [lit., have encircled] the sky in their flock and give [lit., have given] songs, not [lit., hardly] otherwise do your ships [lit., prows] and the young men of your people either hold the port or enter the harbors in full sail. Just proceed and direct [your] step where the way leads you."

She spoke, and, turning away, she shone from her rosy neck, and [her] ambrosial tresses breathed a divine fragrance from the top [of her head]; her robe flowed to the bottoms of [her] feet, and the goddess was revealed through her true gait. When he recognized his mother, that one followed her as she fled [lit., fleeing] with such a voice [i.e., with such words]: "Why do you—you also cruel [i.e., to me]—deceive [your] son so often with false images? Why is it not granted to join right hand to right hand, and to hear and give back [i.e., respond with] true voices?" With such [words] he reproaches [her] and directs [his] step to the walls. But Venus enclosed them as they proceeded [lit., proceeding] with a dark mist, and the goddess poured around [i.e., surrounded] [them] with a great cloak of cloud, lest anyone [be able] to see them and lest anyone be able to touch [them] or to effect a delay or to ask the reasons for coming. She herself went away on high to Paphus and happy [i.e., happily] revisited her home, where [there is] a temple to her, and a hundred altars burn with Sabaean incense and are fragrant with fresh wreaths.

1.418–40
Meanwhile, they took up the road, wherever the path shows [itself], and

presently they were climbing the hill, which looms very great over the city, and which looks from above at the citadels opposite. Aeneas marvels at the mass [or construction] [i.e., of the city], formerly huts, [and] marvels at the gates and the noise and the beds of roads. Burning [i.e., with eagerness] the Tyrians press on: some extended [or were eager to extend] the walls and fortified [or were eager to fortify] the citadel and rolled rocks up[hill] with [their] hands, some chose [or were eager to choose] a place for a building and enclosed [or were eager to enclose] it with a furrow; they select laws and magistracies and a revered senate. Here, some excavate the ports; here, others place the lofty foundations for theaters, and cut huge columns out of the cliffs, tall adornments for future stages. Just as work busies the bees under the sun in early summer through flowery country regions, when they bring forth the full-grown offspring of the race, or when they stuff the dripping honey [i.e., into the comb] and stretch the cells with sweet nectar, or receive the burdens of those coming, or, lined up in a row [lit., a line having been made], they ward off the drones, a lazy bunch [lit., swarm], from the hives; the work heats up and the fragrant honey smells of thyme. "O fortunate ones, whose walls now rise!," says Aeneas, and he looks up at the heights of the city. He bears himself along wrapped in a cloud (marvelous to tell!) through their midst, and mixes with the men and is not seen by anyone.

1.441–93

There was a grove in the middle of the city, most abundant in [its] shade, in which place first the Phoenicians, having been tossed [i.e., ashore] by waves and whirlwind, dug up a token which queen Juno had shown [to them], the head of a fierce horse; for thus [it was shown that] they would now be a people outstanding in war and easy to sustain through the centuries. Here Sidonian Dido was building a huge temple to Juno, rich in gifts and in the power of the goddess, from the steps of which brazen threshholds were rising, and the beams [were] fastened with bronze, [and] the hinge on [or of] the bronze doors grated. The new thing presented [to him] for the first time in this grove soothed [his] fear, here for the first time Aeneas dared to hope for safety and, things having been shattered, to trust better [or to trust better in the things that had been shattered]. For while he scans separate things beneath [the eaves of] the huge temple, waiting for the queen, while he wonders what fortune the city has [lit., what fate there is to the city], and at the [work of the] hands of the craftsmen [competing] among themselves and at the effort of the deeds [or work], he sees the Trojan battles in order and the wars already [or by now] published by rumor through the whole world, [he sees] the sons of Atreus and Priam and Achilles cruel to both [sides]. He halted and, crying, says, "What place now, Achates, what region on earth [is] not full of our struggle? Look—[there is] Priam. Praise has its rewards even here [lit., its own rewards are for praise], there are tears for things and mortal matters touch the mind. Dismiss [your] fears; this story will bring some safety to you." Thus he speaks, and he feeds his mind on the empty image, lamenting much, and he moistens his face with a plentiful river [i.e., of tears]. For he saw how the Greeks, fighting around Troy, fled here, [and how] the Trojan youth pressed, [how] the Phrygians [fled] there, [and how] plumed Achilles pressed on in/with [his] chariot. And crying, he recognizes not far from here the tents of Rhesus with [their] snow-white canvas[es], which, having been betrayed in first sleep, the bloody son of Tydeus [Diomedes] laid waste with much slaughter, and he turned the eager horses aside into the camps before they had tasted the pastures of Troy and had drunk the [river] Xanthus. In another part, Troilus fleeing, [his] weapons having been lost, a boy unfortunate and unequal to, [and] having met Achilles [in battle], is drawn by horses and, on his back, clings to the empty chariot, holding the reins nonetheless. This one's neck and hair are dragged along the ground, and the dust is marked by [his] inverted spear. Meanwhile, to the temple of not-impartial Pallas went the Trojan women, their hair disheveled, and in supplication they carried a robe, sad[ly] and beating [their] breasts with [their] hands [lit., beaten with respect to their breasts by their hands]. The goddess, having turned away, kept her eyes fixed on the ground [or the goddess, having turned her eyes away, held them fixed on the ground]. Three times around the Trojan walls Achilles had dragged Hector, and he was selling the lifeless body for gold. Then indeed he gives a huge groan from his deep heart, as he looked upon the spoils, as [he looked upon] the chariots, as [he looked upon] the body itself of his friend, and Priam reaching out hands without weapons. He recognized himself, too, mixed in with the Achaean leaders, and the battle lines of Dawn [i.e., from the land of dawn, or the East] and the weapons of black Memnon. Raging Penthesilea leads the battle lines of Amazons with [their] crescent-shaped shields, and she blazes in the middle of thousands, a woman warrior fastening beneath her exposed breast golden belts, and [though] a maiden she dares to fight with men.

1.494–519

While these things appear to Dardanian Aeneas to be marvelled at, while he stands agape and clings fastened on one view, the queen proceeds to the temple, Dido, most beautiful in appearance, with a great band of youths thronging about. Just as [when] Diana trains [her] choruses on the banks of Eurotas or along the ridges of Cynthus, [Diana] whom a thousand mountain nymphs follow [lit., having followed] and are gathered from this side and that: she bears a quiver on her shoulder and, stepping, surpasses all the [other] goddesses (joys possess the silent heart of Latona): such was Dido, so she carried herself, happy, urging on the work and the future kingdoms through the midst [of those about her]. Then at the doors of the goddess, in the middle of the vault of the temple, surrounded by weapons and resting high on her throne she sat. She gave rights and laws to men, and she equalized the labor of the works in equal parts or drew [the work assignments] by lot—when suddenly Aeneas sees approaching in a great crowd Antheus and Sergestus and brave Cloanthus and others of the Trojans, whom the black whirlwind at sea had driven apart and had deep within carried to other shores. At once he himself stood agape, at once Achates [was] struck with both happiness and fear; eager, they burned [with desire] to join right [hands]; but the unknown situation disturbs [their] minds. They disguise [their eagerness] and, enclosed in a hollow cloud, they watch [to learn] what fate the men have [lit., what fate (there is) to the men], on what shore they are leaving the fleet, why they are coming; for having been chosen from all the ships they went begging [i.e., to beg] a favor and sought the temple with a shout.

AENEID 2.1–56

2.1–39

All became silent and intent[ly] held [their] faces [on Aeneas]. Thereupon father Aeneas began thus from the high couch: "Unspeakable, queen, [is the] grief you order [me] to renew, how the Danaans [Greeks] overthrew the Trojan power[s] and pitiable kingdom, and the very wretched things which I myself saw and of which I was a great part. What [soldier] of the Myrmidons or Dolopes or what soldier of harsh Ulysses could refrain from tears in telling such things? Even now damp night hastens from [in] the heaven[s] and the falling stars urge sleep. But if [your] desire [is] so great to learn of our misfortunes and briefly to hear the final struggle of Troy, although [my] mind shudders to recall and retreats in grief, I shall begin. Broken in war and driven back by the fates, the leaders of the Greeks, with so many years even then gliding by, with the divine skill of Pallas build a horse the likeness of a mountain, and they weave the ribs with [pieces of] cut fir. They pretend [that this is] a votive offering for [their] return home; this rumor spreads abroad. In this place, having drawn lots, they shut the chosen bodies of men in the dark flank, and fill the huge caverns and belly within with armed soldiery.

There is in view Tenedos, an island most renowned in fame, rich in resources while the kingdom[s] of Priam remained, now only a bay and an anchorage not trustworthy for keels [i.e., ships]. Having been carried to this point they hide themselves on the deserted shore. We thought [they] had gone and had sought Mycenae with the wind. Therefore, all Troy releases itself from long grief: the gates are spread open, it is pleasing to go and to see the Doric camps and the deserted places and abandoned shore: here [stayed] the band of the Dolopes; here cruel Achilles used to exercise; here [was] the place for the fleets, [and] here they used to fight in the line of battle. Some stand agape at the fatal gift of virginal Minerva and marvel at the mass of horse; and Thymoetes first of all urges [that it be] brought within the walls and located on the citadel, whether through deceit or whether the fates of Troy were already tending thus [i.e., in this direction]. But Capys, and [those] in whose mind the common sense was better [lit., to the minds of whom there was better sense], order [them] to hurl down the ambush of the Greeks and the suspicious gifts into the sea and to burn [the horse] with flames placed beneath, or to pierce the hollows of the belly and to examine the hiding places. The uncertain crowd is split into opposite desires.

2.40–56

Then first before [them] all, with a great band accompanying [him], Laocoon, ablaze [i.e., crazed with emotion] runs down from the highest citadel, and from afar [says]: 'O unfortunate citizens, what [is this] so great madness? Do you believe that the enemies [have been] carried away? Or do you think that any gifts of the Greeks are lacking in tricks? Thus is Ulysses known [i.e., is Ulysses famous for *not* being tricky]? Either the Greeks are hidden shut up in this lumber, or this device has been built [to go] against our walls, in order to look down upon [our] homes and to come upon the city from above, or some [other] trick lies hidden; do not trust in the horse, Teucrians [Trojans]. Whatever it is, I fear the Greeks, even [those] bearing gifts.' Having spoken thus, with mighty strength he hurled a huge spear into the flank and into the belly of the beast, curved with joints. That [spear] stood fixed, quivering, and in the shaken belly the hollow cavities resounded and gave a groan. And, if the fates of the gods, if [their] intention had not been ill-omened, he [would have] compelled [us] to defile the Argive hiding places with iron, and Troy would now stand, and you would remain, lofty citadel of Priam.

AENEID 2.199–297

2.199–227

Here something greater and much more to be trembled at is presented to [us] unfortunate ones [i.e., to us Trojans], and disturbs [our] heedless hearts. Laocoon, priest for Neptune chosen by lot, was sacrificing a huge bull at the solemn altars. But behold!—from Tenedos twin snakes with immense coils (I shudder recalling [this]) across the peaceful depths loom over the sea and head for the shores side by side; of which [i.e., of these] the breasts, raised [high] among the waves, and blood-red crests surmount the seas; the other part [i.e., of the snakes' bodies] skims the sea behind and twists the huge backs in a coil. [As] the salt-sea [is] foaming a sound is made; and now they were taking hold of the fields and, their blazing eyes suffused [lit., suffused in respect to their flaming eyes] with blood and fire, they licked their hissing mouths with vibrating tongues. Pale, we fled from the sight [*or* made pale at the sight, we fled]. Those [snakes] pursue Laocoon in a fixed line; and first of all, each serpent, having embraced the small bodies of the two sons [i.e., of Laocoon], entwines [them] and feeds on [the] pitiable limbs with [its] bite; afterwards, they seize [Laocoon] himself approaching as help and bearing weapons, and bind [him] with huge coils; and now, having wrapped him in the middle twice, twice having placed their scaly bodies around his neck, they tower over [him] with [their] head[s] and lofty necks. At that very moment that one [i.e., Laocoon] tries to pull apart the knots with [his] hands, his headbands soaked [lit., having been soaked with respect to his headbands] with gore and black poison, at that very moment he raises horrifying cries to the stars. Of such a sort [is] the mooing, when a wounded bull flees the altar and has shaken from [his] neck the ill-aimed axe. But in a glide [*or* by means of gliding] the twin snakes escape to the highest shrines and seek the citadel of the cruel Tritonian [i.e., Minerva], and beneath the feet of the goddess and beneath the circle of [her] shield they are hidden.

2.228–67

Then to be sure a new fear creeps through the terrified hearts in [us] all, and they say that Laocoon deserving[ly] paid for a crime [lit., deserving paid for a crime], who [because he] wounded the oak [i.e., the horse] with a lance and hurled a wicked spear into/at [the horse's] back. They shout in unison that the image is to be led to the seats [of the gods] and that the powers of the goddess are to be entreated.

We split the ramparts and spread open the walls of the city. All equip [themselves] for the task and put glidings of wheels [i.e., gliding wheels] beneath the feet [of the horse], and extend hempen cables from [or to] the neck; the deadly device scales the walls, pregnant with weapons. Boys and unwed girls sing holy things [i.e., sacred songs] around [the horse] and delight to touch the rope with [their] hand[s]; that [device] goes up and glides, threatening the middle of the city. O homeland! O Ilium, home of the gods, and Trojans' walls, famed in war! Four times on the threshold itself of the gate it resisted, and four times the weapons gave forth a sound from the belly; we press on nonetheless, heedless and blinded by madness, and we set the unlucky omen on the hallowed citadel. Even then for the purpose [or by means] of the fates to come Cassandra discloses words [lit., mouths] not ever, by the order of a god, believed by [us] Trojans. We unfortunates, for whom that day was to be the last, deck the shrines of the gods with festive foliage through the city.

Meanwhile, heaven revolves [lit., is rolled] and night rushes from Ocean, wrapping the earth and sky and tricks of the Myrmidons in great shadow. Spread along the walls, the Trojans fell silent; sleep embraces [their] weary limbs. And now the Argive phalanx, [with] the ships having been arrayed, was going from Tenedos through the friendly silence[s] of the quiet moon seeking the familiar shore[s], when the royal ship [i.e., the ship of the Greek leader Agamemnon] had raised [signal-]flames, and protected by the unfair fates of the gods Sinon stealthily releases the Greeks shut up in the [horse's] belly and the bolts of pine. Having been opened, the horse restores them to the breezes, and happy [i.e., happily] they bring themselves forth from the hollow oak—the leaders Thessandrus and Sthenelus, and dreadful Ulysses, having slipped down the rope [that had been] let down, and Acamas and Thoas and Neoptolemus son of the son of Peleus, and excellent Machaon and Menelaus and Epeos himself, the maker of the trick. They invade the city buried in sleep and wine; the sentinels are killed, and with [or through] the gates lying open they receive all [their] allies and join [to themselves] the confederate battle forces.

2.268–97

It was the time when first quiet begins for wretched mortals and, [as] a gift from the gods, creeps up, most pleasing[ly]. Behold!—in sleep, most miserable Hector seemed to me to be present, before [my] eyes, and to pour out copious tears, as once [he was] dragged by [the] two-horse chariot, and black with bloody dust and pierced [with] a thong through his swollen feet. Woe to me! Of such a sort was he, how much changed from that Hector who returned clothed in the spoils of Achilles, or having flung Phrygian fire[s] on the ships of the Danaans [Greeks]; bearing a filthy beard, and locks matted with blood, and those wounds, a very great number of which he received around [his] homeland's walls. Weeping voluntarily, I myself seemed to address the man and to bring forth mournful words: 'O light of Troy, O most faithful hope of the Teucrians [Trojans], what so great delays have kept [you]? From what shores do you come, Hector, eagerly awaited? How [gladly] we, exhausted, look upon you, after many deaths of your people, after the various struggles of men and of the city! What undeserved cause has befouled [your] peaceful countenance[s]? Or why do I see these wounds?' He [answered] nothing, nor does he delay me asking empty things [i.e., vainly], but grievously drawing groans from his deep heart he says, 'Alas, [child] born from a goddess, flee, and snatch yourself from these flames. The enemy holds the ramparts; Troy rushes downward from [its] lofty summit. Enough [has been] given to the homeland and to Priam; if Troy were able to be defended by [any] hand, it would indeed have been defended by this [one]. Troy entrusts [her] holy things [i.e., rituals] and her household gods to you; take these [as] companions of [your] fates, seek for these great walls, which you will establish at last, the sea having been thoroughly wandered.' Thus he speaks, and with his hands he carries forth from the innermost sanctuaries the headbands and powerful Vesta and the eternal flame.

AENEID 2.469–566

2.469–525

Before the entry itself and on the first threshold Pyrrhus leaps up, flashing with weapons and bronze light: just as when a serpent, having eaten evil plants, [a serpent] that, swollen, the cold midwinter was hiding beneath the earth, now new, its skin having been set aside and sleek with youth, rolls its slippery back[s] into the light, tall, its breast raised towards the sun, and flashes from its mouth with its three-forked tongue[s]. At the same time huge Periphas and the driver of Achilles' horses, the armorbearer Automedon, at the same time all the Scyrian youth approach the building and toss flames toward the roofs. A two-headed axe having been snatched up, he himself breaks through the hard doorway[s] among the first men and tears the bronze doorposts from the hinge. And now, the timber having been destroyed, he hollowed out the solid oak and gave [i.e., created] a huge opening with a wide mouth. The house within appears, and the long forecourts are revealed, the inner chamber of Priam and of the former kings appears, and they see armed men standing on the first threshold. But the inner house is confused with lament and wretched uproar, and the vaulted halls within wail with feminine shrieks; the uproar strikes the golden stars. Then the trembling mothers [i.e., women] wander in the huge halls, and having embraced the doorposts they hold [them] and fasten kisses [on them]. Pyrrhus presses on with [his] father's force [i.e., strength inherited from his father]; neither the bolts nor the sentinels themselves are able to withstand [him]; the door totters with [the] repeated battering ram, and having been moved from the hinge the doorposts fall forward. A path is made by force; having been let in, the Greeks burst [through] the entrances and slaughter the first [men] and fill the places far and wide with soldiery. Not thus, when a frothy stream has gone forth, [its] dikes having been broken, and has overcome the opposing structures with [its] whirlpool, is it carried raging into the fields in a mass and does it drag the herds, together with [their] stables, through all the fields. I myself saw Neoptolemus raging with slaughter and the twin sons of Atreus on the threshold, I saw Hecuba and a hundred daughters and daughters-in-law, and Priam by the altars polluting with blood the fires which he himself had consecrated. Those famed fifty marriage chambers, the [so] great expectation of descendants, the doorposts proud with barbarian gold and spoils, fell forward; the Greeks hold [the palace] where the fire fails.

And perhaps you may/might ask what the fates of Priam were. When he saw the fall of the captured city and the shattered doorways of the house[s] and the enemy in the middle of the inner chamber[s], the old man vainly places around [his] shoulders trembling with age the long-unaccustomed weapons [i.e., the weapons which he had not used for a long time, since he had been young and strong] and is girded [i.e., girds himself] with the useless iron, and is carried into the crowded enemies, about to die. In the middle of the home [i.e., palace] and under the bare axis of heaven there was a huge altar and next [to it] a very old laurel tree, leaning over the altar and embracing the household gods in [its] shade. Here sat Hecuba and the daughters, crowded around the altars in vain, like doves driven headlong by a black storm, and embracing the images of the gods. But as she saw Priam himself, [his] youthful weapons having been taken up, she said, 'What [so] dreadful intention, most wretched spouse, has driven [you] to be girded [i.e., to gird yourself] with these weapons? Or where do you rush? The occasion does not require such help nor these protectors of yours; no, [not] if my Hector himself were now present. Finally, then, come to this place; this altar will protect [us] all, or you will die together [with us].' Having spoken thus with [her] mouth she received [him] to herself [i.e., she took him into her arms] and placed the aged man on the holy seat.

2.526–66

But look!—Polites, one of the sons of Priam, having escaped from the slaughter of [i.e., performed by] Pyrrhus, flees through the weapons, through the enemies in the long porticoes, and, wounded, surveys the empty halls. Blazing with a hostile wound [i.e., with the intention of inflicting a hostile wound], Pyrrhus pursues, and now is just about to [lit., and now, now] take [him] with his hand and press [him] with the spear. Finally, as he came forth before the eyes and faces of [his] parents, he fell, and poured forth [his] life with much blood. Here, Priam, although he is already held in the midst of death [i.e., although he is already half dead], nevertheless did not restrain [himself] nor did he spare voice and wrath: 'For [this] crime, for such deeds dared, may the gods (if there is any [sense of] loyalty in heaven to care for such things) pay in full deserved thanks and render the rewards owed to you, [you] who have made me see the death of [my] son before my own face [lit., in my presence] and who have defiled [his] parents' faces with death,' he exclaims. 'But that famous Achilles, from whom you lie that you [were] born, was not such a man in [the case of his] enemy Priam; but he blushed [i.e., with reverence] at the rights and faith of a suppliant, and returned Hector's lifeless body for burial [lit., for the tomb] and sent me back into my kingdom[s].' Thus spoke the old man, and hurled his weapon, harmless and without a blow, that [was] immediately repelled by the clanging bronze and hung in vain from the top of the boss of the shield. To this man Pyrrhus [said]: 'You will carry back these [words], then, and will go as a messenger to [my] father, the son of Peleus. Remember to report to that one my sorrowful deeds and degenerate Neoptolemus. Now, die.' Saying this, he drew the man trembling and slipping in the abundant blood of [his] son to the altars themselves, and he entwined [Priam's] hair in [his] left hand, and with [his] right hand he took out [his] flashing sword and buried it up to the hilt in [Priam's] side. This [was] the end of the fates of Priam, this destruction [over]took him, once the ruler of Asia, proud with so many peoples and lands, as he watched [lit., seeing] Troy burned and Pergamon fallen. [His] huge body lies on the shore, and the head torn from the shoulders and the corpse without a name.

But then for the first time fierce horror surrounded me. I was dazed; the image of [my] dear father rose up [i.e., before me], as I saw the king of equal age breathing out [his] life because of [*or* from] a cruel wound, forsaken Creusa [i.e., her image] rose up, and the ravaged house and the misfortune of little Iulus. I look back and survey what forces there are around me. Exhausted, they all [had] deserted [me], and with a jump sent [their] wretched bodies to the earth or gave [them] to the fires.

AENEID 2.735–804

2.735–67

Here some [lit., I don't know what] unfriendly divinity stole [my] confused mind from me in my agitation [lit., from me agitated]. For while I am following out-of-the-way [places] at a run [i.e., by running] and am leaving the known area of roads, alas!—whether [my] wife Creusa halted, [and was] snatched by a wretched fate, or wandered from the way, or sat down, having fallen, [is] uncertain; nor [was] she returned to our eyes afterwards. Nor did I look back at her, having been lost, or turn back [my] attention [to her], before we came to the mound and sacred home of ancient Ceres; here, all finally having been gathered together, one was missing, and she eluded [her] companions, [her] son, and [her] husband. Whom of both men and gods did I not accuse, mad[ly], or what more cruel thing did I see in the overthrown city? I entrust Ascanius, father Anchises, and the Teucrian [Trojan] Penates to [my] allies, and hide [them] in the winding valley; I myself seek the city again and gird myself [lit., am girded] with shining arms. It is decided [lit., (the opinion) stands] to renew all [our] misfortunes and to turn back through all [of] Troy and again to expose myself [lit., (my) head] to dangers. First I seek again the ramparts and the dark thresholds of the gate, where I had carried out [my] step [i.e., where I had exited the city], and through the night I follow backwards the footprints [having been] observed and I survey [everything] with [my] eye[s] [lit., light]. [There is] terror everywhere in/for [my] mind, [and] at the same time the silences themselves are terrifying. Thence I take myself home, if perchance, perchance, she had gone [lit., carried her foot] [there]; the Danaans [Greeks] had rushed in and [now] held the whole house. At once devouring fire rolls [lit., is rolled] to the highest rafters/summits by the wind; the flames overwhelm [the house], the heat rages to the breezes. I advance and visit again the home and citadel of Priam; and now Phoenix and terrible Ulysses, [having been] chosen [as] guards, were guarding the booty in the empty porticoes, the sanctuary of Juno. To this place from all sides Trojan treasure snatched out of burnt shrines, and the tables of the gods and the wine craters of solid gold [lit., solid from gold], and the captive clothing is heaped up. Boys and trembling mothers stand round in a long row.

2.768–804

Having dared in fact even to utter words through the shadow[s] I filled the streets with shouting, and sorrowful[ly] I called Creusa again and again, repeating [her name] in vain. The sad image and shade of Creusa herself, and a form larger than [that I had] known, appeared to me before my eyes [as I was] seeking and rushing in the dwellings of the city without end. I stood in a daze, and [my] hair[s] stood [i.e., on end] and [my] voice stuck in [my] throat. Then she [seemed to] speak and to take away [my] cares with these words: 'Why, o sweet husband, is it pleasing [to you] to indulge so much in crazed grief? These things do not happen without the divine influence of the gods; nor is it right for you to take Creusa [as] a companion from here, [n]or does the famous ruler of lofty Olympus allow [it]. Long exiles [are in store] for you, and the vast surface of the sea must be plowed, and you will come [to] the land [of] Hesperia, where the Lydian Tiber flows in a gentle stream [lit., line] between rich fields of men. There, fortunate affairs and a kingdom and a royal spouse [will be] won by you; dismiss [your] tears for beloved Creusa. I shall not see the lofty homes of the Myrmidons or Dolopes, [n]or will I, a Trojan woman and daughter-in-law of divine Venus, go to be a slave to Greek matrons [i.e., mothers]. Rather, the great mother of the gods detains me on these shores. And now, farewell, and preserve the love for our shared child [i.e., the child we share].' When she gave these words, she left [me] crying and wishing to say many things, and she withdrew into the thin breezes. Three times [I] tried to put [my] arms around [her] neck there, three times the image, grasped in vain, escaped [my] hands, like light winds and most similar to winged sleep. So at last I see [my] allies again, the night having been consumed.

And marvelling, I discover here that a huge number of new companions has flowed together, both mothers and men, young men gathered for exile, a wretched crowd. They came together from all sides, prepared in minds and resources, to launch [ships] on the sea for whatever lands I might wish. And now the morning star was rising from the ridges of lofty Ida and was leading [forth] day, and the Danaans [Greeks] were holding the besieged thresholds of the gates, nor was any hope of help given. I withdrew and, [my] father having been picked up, I sought the mountains.

AENEID 4.1–449

4.1–53

But the queen, hurt for some time now by a grievous care, nourishes the wound in [her] veins and is consumed by blind fire [i.e., passion]. The great [lit., much] bravery of the man and the great [lit., much] honor of [his] people come back to [her] mind; [his] appearance[s] and words cling fixed in [her] heart, and [her] care does not give peaceful rest to [her] limbs. The next Aurora [i.e., dawn] was traversing the lands with [her] Phoebean [i.e., Apollonian] torch and had removed the dewy shadow from the heaven, when the scarcely rational [woman] addresses her likeminded sister thus: "Sister Anna, what dreams terrify me, suspended [i.e., in fear]! Who [is] this new stranger [who] has come to our home, bearing himself as what a person in appearance, with how brave a heart and weapons [or shoulders/arms]! Indeed, I believe, nor [is my] belief groundless, that [his] race is of the gods. Fear proves [i.e., is the proof of] ignoble minds. Alas, by what fates [has] that man [been] tossed about! Of what exhausted [i.e., draining] wars he was singing! If it did not remain fixed and immovable in my mind [lit., to me in mind] not to desire to unite myself to anyone in [or by means of] a conjugal bond, after [my] first love cheated [me], having been deceived, with death; if it had not wearied me of wedding chamber and wedding torch, to this one weakness perhaps I was [i.e., would have been] able to succumb. Anna—I shall confess truly—after the fates [i.e., death] of [my] poor husband Sychaeus and the household gods sprinkeld with [my] brother's slaughter [i.e., the murder of my husband by my brother], this man alone has turned [my] senses and has struck [my] wavering mind. I recognize the traces of the old flame [i.e., passion]. But I would hope that either the deep earth would gape open for me first or that the all-powerful father would drive me to the shadows with [his] lightning bolt, [to] the pallid shadows in Erebus and the deep night, before, honor, I violate you or relax your decrees [i.e., loosen (the hold of) your decrees on me]. That man who first joined me to him stole away my love[s]; let him have [it] with him and preserve [it] in the tomb." Having spoken thus she filled the fold [of her garment] with the tears having sprung up.

Anna responds: "O, more beloved by [your] sister than the light [i.e., of life itself], grieving alone in continual youth [i.e., throughout your young womanhood] will you be consumed, and will you know neither sweet children nor the rewards of Venus [i.e., love]? Do you believe that the ashes or the buried souls of the dead care about this? So be it; once upon a time, no suitors moved [you], wretched [as you were], not in Libya, not previously in Tyre; Iarbas [was] despised [i.e., by you], and the other leaders, whom the African land, rich in triumphs, nourishes; will you resist even a pleasing love? And does it not come into [your] mind in whose fields you have settled?

On/from this side, the Gaetulian cities, a people unconquerable in war, and the unbridled Numidians and unfriendly Syrtis surround [you]; on/from this side [is] a region forsaken to/on account of drought, and the Barcaeans, raging far and wide. Why should I mention the wars arising from Tyre and the threats of [your] brother? Indeed, I think that with gods being [i.e., as] guides and Juno [being] favorable the Ilian [i.e., Trojan] ships held [their] course [here] [lit., this course] by means of/with the wind. What a city [is] this you will see [arise], what kingdoms [you will see] arise from such a union! To what great things [i.e., greatness] will Punic glory raise itself with the arms of the Teucrians [i.e., Trojans] attending! Just ask pardon of the gods, and sacrifices having been performed [or by means of sacrifices performed] indulge hospitality [i.e., show hospitality to your guest] and weave reasons for delay, while winter rages at sea and Orion [is] rainy, and [their] ships [have been] shattered, while the sky [is] not favorable."

4.54–89

With these words she inflamed [Dido's] mind with profound love and gave hope to [her] wavering mind and loosened [her sense of] shame. At first they approach the shrines and seek peace through altars [i.e., by means of sacrifice]; they sacrifice two-year-old sheep chosen in accordance with custom to law-bringing Ceres and Phoebus and father Lyaeus [i.e., Baccus], and to Juno before all, to whom marriage bonds [are] a care. Very beautiful Dido herself, holding the libation bowl in [her] right hand, pours [the offering] in the middle between the horns [lit., in between the middle of the horns] of a shining white heifer, or before the faces of the gods [i.e., of their statues] strides to the rich altars, and she renews the day with gifts, and the hearts of sheep having been revealed, gaping [or gaping at the the hearts revealed], she consults the quivering entrails. Alas, ignorant [are the] minds of prophets! How [do] prayers [help] her raging [in passion], how do shrines [help her]? The flame consumes [her] soft marrow[s] meanwhile, and the silent wound beneath her heart is alive. Unhappy Dido burns [lit., is burned] and in a frenzy roams through the entire city, like a doe, an arrow having been shot, which, unsuspecting, a shepherd, chasing with weapons, has pierced from afar among the Cretan groves, and [in which] he, unaware, has left [his] flying iron. That one wanders through the woods and groves of Mt. Dicte in flight; the death-bringing reed clings to [her] side. Now she brings Aeneas with her through the middle of the walls and shows [him] Sidonian wealth and the city [that has been] prepared, she begins to speak and in the middle of a word she stops; now, the day waning, she seeks out the same banquets, and mad[ly] demands to hear again the Trojan struggles and again hangs on/from the mouth [i.e., words] of [Aeneas] speaking. After[wards], having departed, and the gloomy moon in turn suppresses [its] light and the falling stars suggest sleep, she grieves alone in [her] empty house and lies upon the bed coverings left behind [i.e., by him]. Absent [from him], she hears and sees that man, absent, or seized by the image of [his] father she holds Ascanius in her lap, if [only] she might be able to deceive [her] unspeakable love. The towers [that had been] begun do not rise up, the youth do not exercise [i.e., work out with] weapons, or prepare the ports or battlements, safe [i.e., so as to make them safe] for war; the interrupted projects hang [i.e., wait in suspense] and the huge heights [lit., threats] of the walls, and the scaffolding made equal to the heavens.

4.90–128

As soon as the dear wife of Jupiter realized that [she] [lit., whom; i.e., Dido] was being possessed by such a disease and that [her] reputation did not stand in the way of passion, the Saturnian [goddess] approaches Venus with such words: "Both you and your son win outstanding praise indeed and ample spoils (great and glorious [is] divine power), if one woman has been conquered by the stratagem of two divinities. Nor does it so escape my notice that you, having dreaded our walls, considered the homes of lofty Carthage suspect. But what will be the limit, or where now [are you headed] with such great strife? Why don't we work for eternal peace instead, and the marriage [that we] agreed upon? You have what you sought with all [your] intent: Dido, loving [i.e., in love], burns and has drawn passion through [her] bones. Therefore, let us rule this people in common and with equal powers; let [Dido] be allowed to serve a Phrygian husband and to entrust to your right hand her Tyrians as a dowry."

To that one (for she sensed that [Juno had] spoken with feigned intent, so that she might divert the kingdom of Italy to Libyan shores) Venus proceeded thus in turn: "What crazy person would refuse such things or would prefer to contend with you in war? If only luck may follow the deed that you mention. But I am borne uncertain by the fates [i.e., I am in doubt], whether Jupiter would wish there to be one city for the Tyrians and those having set out from Troy, or would approve that the peoples be combined or agreements [between them] be joined. You [are his] wife, for you it is allowed to test [his] intent by asking. Proceed; I shall follow." Then queenly Juno rejoined thus: "That task will be mine [lit., with me]. Now, how [the matter] at hand [lit., that which presses on (us)] may be accomplished, I shall explain in a few [words]—pay attention. Aeneas and most pitiful Dido are preparing to go into the grove together to hunt, when tomorrow's Titan [i.e., sun] has lifted [lit., will have lifted] [its] first risings and has [lit., will have] uncovered the earth with [its] rays. Onto these [two] I shall pour down from above a cloud, dark with hail mixed in, while the bands of hunters tremble and surround the groves with net[s], and I shall stir up the whole heaven with thunder. [Their] companions will scatter and will be covered by dark night: Dido and the Trojan leader will arrive at the same cave. I shall be present and, if your consent [is] sure with me, I shall join [her to him] in a lasting union and shall proclaim [her] his own. This will be [their] wedding." Not having resisted Juno's request [lit., the one requesting], the Cytherean [goddess] nodded in approval and laughed, the tricks having been revealed.

4.129–72

Meanwhile, Aurora, rising, left Ocean. The chosen youth go [out] from the gates, the light of the sun having risen, the wide-meshed nets, snares, hunting spears with broad iron [i.e., blade], and the Massylian horsemen rush forth and the keen-scented strength of dogs [i.e., a pack of keen-scented dogs]. The first men of the Phoenicians await at the thresholds the queen, delaying in the bedchamber, and [the horse] of resounding hoof stands, outstanding in both purple and gold, and fierce[ly] chomps on the foaming reins. Finally she comes forth, with a great troop surrounding [her], having been encircled [i.e., clothed] in [lit., with respect to] a Sidonian mantle with embroidered border; her [lit., whose] quiver [is] of gold; [her] tresses are tied into a knot of [lit., into] gold, a golden pin fastens [her] purple garment below. Likewise both the Phrygian [i.e., Trojan] comrades and joyful Iulus also go forth. Aeneas himself, most handsome before all the others, carries himself [as] a companion and brings together the lines [i.e., of hunters]. As when Apollo leaves wintry Lycia and the streams of Xanthus and looks upon maternal Delos and renews the dancing choruses, and around the altars the Cretans and Dryopes, mixed together, roar, and the tattooed [*or* painted] Agathyrsi; he himself steps on the ridges of Cynthus, and shaping his flowing tresses, he presses [them] with a pliable branch, and entwines [them] with gold, [and his] weapons resound on [his] shoulders; not at all more slow[ly] than that one went Aeneas, so much beauty shines from his noble face. After they came [lit., it was come] into the tall mountains and the pathless lairs, behold!—wild she-goats, dislodged from the top of a rock, ran along the mountain ridges; in another area, stags cross the open plains in a run, and fill dusty lines in flight, and leave the mountains. But in the middle of the glades, the boy Ascanius delights in [his] keen horse and now pursues these [i.e., the latter] at a run, now passes those [i.e., the former], and hopes for a foaming boar to be given to [his] prayers [i.e., to him] amidst the lazy herds, or for a tawny lion to descend from the mountain.

Meanwhile, the heaven begins to be confused with a great rumble, a stormcloud follows with hail mixed in, and in all directions the Tyrian comrades and the Trojan youth and the Dardanian descendant of Venus [i.e., Ascanius] in fear sought different covers [i.e., places of cover] through the fields; the streams rush down from the mountains. Dido and the Trojan leader arrive at the same cave. Earth first and attendant Juno give a signal; fires and the upper air, witness to the union, flashed, and the nymphs shrieked on the highest peak. That day [was] the first [cause] of death and the first cause of evils; for neither by appearance nor by reputation is Dido moved, nor does she now ponder a secret love; she calls [this] marriage, she cloaks [her] fault with this name.

4.173–218

Immediately Rumor goes through the great cities of Libya, Rumor, than which no other evil [lit., bad thing] is swifter: she thrives on movement and acquires strength by going, small at first on account of fear, [but] soon she raises herself into the air[s] and steps on the earth and hides [her] head among the clouds. Parent Earth, as they report, provoked by wrath for the gods, gave birth to that [one] last [i.e., of the gods], a sister to Coeus and Enceladus, swift in respect to [her] feet and with swift wings, a dreadful portent, huge; as many feathers as there are to her [lit., to whom] with respect to her body, [there are] so many wakeful eyes beneath (marvelous to tell), as many tongues, as many mouths resound, she raises as many ears. At night she flies in the middle of [i.e., between] heaven and earth, rustling through the shadow, nor does she turn down [her] eyes in sweet sleep; in the light she sits [as] a guardian either at the top of the highest roof or in tall towers, and terrorizes great cities, as greedy a messenger of the false and perverse as of the true. This one, then, rejoicing, filled the peoples with varied talk, and proclaimed equally things done and undone: that Aeneas, born from Trojan blood, had come, to whom as husband fair Dido deigns to join herself; that now through the winter, however long it may be, they caress each other in luxury, forgetful of [their] kingdoms and seized with shameful desire. The loathsome goddess spreads these things everywhere to the mouths of men. Straightaway she turns her path[s] to king Iarbas, and inflames his mind with words and increases [his] anger[s].

This one, born from Ammon, a Garamantian nymph having been raped, [erected] a hundred huge temples to Jove in [his] broad kingdoms, erected a hundred altars, and with the blood of sheep had consecrated the watchful fire, eternal sentinel[s] of the gods, the fertile earth, and the thresholds flowering with varied wreaths. And crazed of mind and inflamed by bitter rumor, this one is said to have beseeched Jupiter greatly [lit., many things] [as] a suppliant, with hands upturned before the altars in the midst of the presence[s] of the gods: "All-powerful Jupiter, to whom now the Maurusian [i.e., Moorish] people, having dined on embroidered couches, pour [as a libation] Lenaean [i.e., Bacchic] honor [i.e., wine, the manifestation of Bacchus], do you see these things? Or, father, when you hurl [your] lightning bolts, do we quake at you in vain, and do blind fires in the clouds terrify the minds [of men] and stir up empty rumblings? The woman who, wandering in our territories, set up a small city at a price, to whom [we gave] a shore for plowing and to whom we gave the laws of the place, has rejected our marriage alliances and has received Aeneas [as] master into [her] kingdoms. And now, that Paris, with [his] effeminate retinue, having tied a Maeonian cap on [i.e., under] his chin and perfumed hair [lit., having been tied below his chin and perfumed hair with the Maeonian cap], has possession of the object taken; we, to be sure, bring gifts to your temples, and cherish an empty rumor."

4.219–95

The all-powerful one heard [him] praying with such words and holding the altars, and he twisted [his] eyes to the royal walls and to the lovers forgetful of [lit., having forgotten] [their] better reputation. Then he addresses Mercury thus and entrusts such things [i.e., words] [to him]: "Come now, son, call the West winds and glide on wings and address the Dardanian leader, who now lingers in Tyrian Carthage and does not look toward the cities given by the fates, and carry my words down through the swift breezes. [His] most beautiful mother did not promise us that that [man was] such a man, and [not] for this reason has she rescued [lit., does she rescue] him twice from the weapons of the Greeks; but [she promised that] he would be the sort of man who would rule Italy teeming with power and roaring with war, [who] would produce a people from the lofty blood of Teucer, and [who] would send the whole earth beneath laws. If no glory of such great things inflames [him] and in addition he himself does not pursue an effort on behalf of his own praise, does he [as] father begrudge the Roman citadels to Ascanius? What is he planning? Or with what expectation does he delay in [i.e., among] a hostile people and not look towards Ausonian offspring and the Lavinian fields? Let him sail! This is the chief thing; let this be our message."

He had spoken. That one prepared to obey the command of the great father; and first he fastens golden sandals to [his] feet, which carry him aloft with wings above either the seas or land with swift blast. Then he takes a wand: with this that one summons forth pale souls from Orcus, [and] sends others beneath gloomy Tartarus [i.e., Hades], he gives sleep and takes [it] away, and seals the eyes with death [or releases the eyes from death]. Relying on that [wand] he drives the winds and swims across stormy clouds. And now, flying, he sees the head and steep flanks of harsh Atlas who supports the heaven on his peak, of Atlas, whose pine-bearing head, bound continually [i.e., thickly] with black clouds, is beaten by both wind and rain, [and] snow, having been poured on [his] shoulders, covers [them], then streams rush headlong from the chin of the old man, and [his] bristling beard is stiff with ice. The Cyllenean, resting first on even wings, stood here; from here he hurled himself headlong with his entire body to the waves like a bird, which flies low around the shores, around the fish-filled rocks, close to the seas. Hardly otherwise was he flying between lands and heaven to the sandy shore of Libya, and coming from [his] maternal grandfather [i.e., Atlas] the Cyllenean offspring was cutting through the winds. As soon as he touched the huts with his winged soles [i.e., feet], he spies Aeneas building citadels and making shelters. And to that one there was [i.e., he had] a sword spangled with tawny jasper, and a cloak let down from his shoulders was bright with Tyrian purple, which wealthy Dido had made [as] a gift, and she had separated the webs [i.e., she had woven into the fabric] with slender gold [thread]. Straightaway he addresses [him]: "Are you now laying the foundations of lofty Carthage and, wife-ruled, do you build up a lovely city? Alas, [you], having forgotten the kingdom and your affairs! The ruler himself of the gods, who turns the heaven and lands with [his] power, sends me to you from bright Olympus; he himself orders [me] to bear these commands through the swift breezes: What are you planning? Or with what expectation do you waste times of idleness in Libyan lands? If no glory of such great affairs moves you [and in addition you yourself do not pursue an effort on behalf of your own praise], consider Ascanius rising up and the hopes for [your] heir Iulus, to whom the kingdom of Italy and the Roman land is owed." Having spoken with such a speech the Cyllenean left mortal view[s] in the middle of [his] speech and from afar disappeared from [Aeneas'] eyes into thin air.

But Aeneas stood speechless indeed, frenzied at/by the sight, and [his] hair stood on end from horror and [his] voice stuck in [his] jaws. He is eager to depart in flight and to leave the sweet lands, stunned by so great a warning and order of the gods. Alas—what should he do? With what [form of] address should he dare to conciliate the raging queen? What first beginnings should he take up? And he divides his swift mind now in this direction now in that, and takes [it] into different directions and revolves [it] through all things. This opinion seemed preferable to him as he wavered [lit., to him wavering]: he calls Mnestheus and Sergestus and strong Serestus, [and orders them to] [lit., that they should] silent[ly] make ready the fleet and drive [their] companions to the shores, prepare weapons and conceal what the reason is for doing things anew; [he decides that] meanwhile, since excellent Dido does not know and does not expect such love[s] to be broken, he himself will test approaches and what times for speaking [are] easiest, what way [is] right for things. Very swiftly all glad[ly] obey the command and fulfill the orders.

4.296–330

But the queen suspects tricks (who could deceive a lover?), and was the first to understand movements about to come, fearing all things, [even] safe ones. The same wicked Rumor brought [to her], raving, [the news that] the fleet was being armed and the way was being prepared. Bereft of [her] mind she rages and rushes, inflamed, through the whole city, like a Bacchant aroused, rituals having been stirred up, when the triennial rites spur her, [the cry] "Bacchus" having been heard, and nocturnal Cithaeron calls [her] with a shout. Finally, she addresses Aeneas voluntarily with these words:

"Treacherous one, did you hope to pretend still that so great a crime was possible and to depart from my land quiet[ly]? Does neither our love, nor the right [hand] once given, nor Dido, about to die from a cruel death, hold you? Aren't you hurrying, in fact, to prepare the fleet under the winter star and to go through the deep in the midst of the North winds, cruel man? What, if you were not seeking foreign fields and unknown homes, and ancient Troy remained, would Troy be sought by the fleets through the wave-filled sea? Are you fleeing me? By these tears and your right hand (since I myself have left nothing else to my now-wretched self), by our marriage[s], by the wedding hymns begun, if I have well deserved anything regarding you, or anything of mine was sweet to you, pity the falling house and discard, I beg you, that intention of yours, if [there is] any place still for prayers. On account of you the Libyan peoples and the rulers of the Nomads hate [me and] the Tyrians [are] hostile; on account of the same you, [my sense of] shame [has been] extinguished, and my earlier reputation, by which alone I was approaching the stars. For what do you, guest (since this name alone remains from [my] husband), desert me, about to die? Why do I delay? Or [am I waiting] until [my] brother Pygmalion destroys my city walls, or Gaetulian Iarbas takes [me] captive? At least, if there had been some progeny begotten to me from you before flight, if some little Aeneas were playing for me in the hall, who at least recalled you in face, I would not indeed seem entirely taken and forsaken."

4.331–92

She had spoken. That one was holding [his] eyes unmoved on account of the warnings of Jupiter, and having struggled, was pressing [his] concern beneath [his] heart. Finally he says a few [words]: "Queen, I shall never deny that you, who are able by speaking to list very many things, [have] deserved [very many things], nor will it displease me to remember Elissa [i.e., Dido] so long as I [am] mindful of myself, so long as breath controls these limbs. I shall say a few things on behalf of [my] case. I neither expected—don't imagine [this]—to hide this escape by stealth, nor did I ever hold out the marriage torches of a husband or come into these agreements. If the fates permitted me to lead a life by my own authority and to calm [my] cares of my own accord, I would [dwell in] the city [of] Troy first of all and would cherish the sweet remnants of my [people], [and] the lofty walls of Priam would remain, and I would have established by [my own] hand a reborn Troy for the conquered. But now, Grynean Apollo [has ordered me to pursue] great Italy, the Lycian lots have ordered [me] to pursue Italy; this [is my] love, this is [my] homeland. If the citadel[s] of Carthage and the sight of the Libyan city detains you, a Phoenician, what [source of] jealousy, then, is it for [i.e., why do you begrudge] the Teucrians to settle in the Ausonian land? It is right for us, too, to seek foreign kingdoms. The troubled image of father Anchises advises and terrifies me in sleep, as often as night covers the lands with damp shadows, as often as the fiery stars rise; [my] son Ascanius [advises] me, and the wrong done to my dear son [lit., the wrong of (his) dear head], whom I am depriving of the kingdom of Hesperia and the fated fields. In fact, now an agent of the gods, sent by Jupiter himself (I swear [on] each head), has carried down [his] orders through the swift breezes: I myself saw the god in the clear light, entering the walls [i.e., of the house] and I drew in [his] voice with these ears. Stop inflaming me and you with your laments; I pursue Italy not of [my own] accord."

Having turned away for some time now she looks at [him] saying such things, turning her eyes [now] here, [now] there, and surveys [him] entire[ly] with silent eyes and, inflamed, speaks thus: "Neither [did] a divine parent for your family nor [did] Dardanus [as] founder [beget you], but the Caucasus rough with hard crags begot you, and Hyrcanian tigers suckled you [lit., moved (their) teats towards (you)]. For why do I pretend otherwise or for what greater [things] do I save myself? Did he lament at our weeping? Did he turn [his] eyes? Did he, won over, cry [lit., give tears] or pity the lover [lit., one loving (him)]? What things shall I set before what things [i.e., what shall I prefer to what]? Now, now neither greatest Juno nor the Saturnian father looks at these things with favorable eyes. [My] trust [is] safe nowhere. I received [him] tossed out on the shore, needy, and foolish[ly] shared my rule with him [lit., established (him) in the part of rule]. I brought back [his] lost fleet [and] allies from death (alas! inflamed by the furies, I am being carried [off]); now prophet Apollo, now the Lycian lots, and now an agent of the gods sent by Jupiter himself brings dreadful orders through the breezes. To the [gods] above, clearly, this is [their] task, this concern troubles [the gods] in their calm [lit., the calm ones]. I neither hold you nor contradict [your] words: go, pursue Italy with the winds, seek kingdoms through the waves. I hope, to be sure, if the faithful gods can [do] anything, that in the middle of the rocks you will drink in [your] punishments and will often call on Dido by name. [Though] absent, I shall pursue [you] with black fires and, when cold death has separated [my] limbs from [my] soul, I shall be present [as] a shade in all places. Cruel man, you will pay the penalty. I shall hear and this report will come to me beneath the deepest souls of the dead." She breaks off her speech in the middle of these words and, sick [at heart], she flees the breezes and turns herself away from [his] eyes and carries [herself] off, leaving [him] hesitating [to say] many things with fear and preparing to say many things. [Her] slaves support [her] and carry her collapsed body [lit., limbs] back to the marble bedchamber and place [her] on the bed[s].

4.393–449

But although he desires to soothe the grieving one by consoling and to turn aside [her] cares with words, moaning much [lit., many things] and shaken in his mind by great love faithful Aeneas nevertheless performs the orders of the gods and returns to the fleet. Then the Teucrians truly urge on [i.e., get to work] and launch the lofty ships on [i.e., along] the whole shore. The prow coated with pitch [lit., anointed] swims, and they bear leafy oars and oaks from the forests, unworked because of their eagerness for flight.

You could see them departing and rushing from the whole city: and just as when ants, mindful of winter, plunder a huge heap of spelt and store [it] in [their] dwelling, the black line [i.e., of ants] goes through the fields and carries the booty through the grasses on a narrow path; some [lit., a part] push huge grains with [their] shoulders, having leaned against [them], some [lit., a(nother) part] drive along the lines and chastise delays, [and] the entire path is busy with work. What sensation was yours [lit., was there to you], Dido, [as you were] observing such things, or what laments did you give forth, when you saw from the top of the citadel that the shores were busy far and wide, and you saw the whole plain before [your] eyes being confused with such great shouts! Wicked Love, what do you not force mortal hearts [to do]! She is driven to go again into tears, to try [him] again with entreating, and [as] a suppliant to submit [her] spirits to love, lest, about to die in vain, she leave anything untried.

"Anna, you see the hurrying-about [lit., that it is hurried about] on the entire shore; they have gathered from all sides; now the linen sail summons the breezes, and the happy sailors have placed wreaths on the sterns. If I have been able to expect this so great grief, I shall be able to endure, too, sister. Nevertheless, carry out this one thing for wretched me, Anna; for that treacherous one cherishes you alone, [and] even entrusts [his] hidden feelings to you; you alone know delicate approaches [i.e., ways to approach] and the [right] times of the man. Go, sister, and [as] a suppliant address the proud stranger: I did not swear with the Greeks at Aulis to destroy the Trojan people [n]or did I send a fleet to Pergamum [i.e., Troy], nor did I tear away the ashes and dead spirit[s] of [his] father Anchises. Why does he refuse to admit my words into [his] harsh ears? Where is he rushing? Let him give this final gift to [his] wretched lover: let him wait for an easy escape and conveying winds. No longer do I ask for the ancient marriage which he betrayed, nor that he be without fair Latium and leave [his] kingdom: I ask for empty time, quiet and a space for [my] madness, until my fate teaches me, conquered, to grieve. I ask this final favor (take pity on [your] sister), which I shall repay heaped up by [or at the time of] death when he has given [it] to me."

She entreated with such [words], and her most wretched sister carries and brings back such weepings. But he is moved by no laments [n]or gently [lit., gentle] hears any words; the fates stand in the way, and the god obstructs the peaceful ears of the man. And just as when the Alpine Northern winds with blasts now from this side now from that struggle amongst themselves to uproot an oak tree sturdy with aged strength; a creaking goes [forth], and the lofty leaves strew the earth, the trunk having been struck; [the oak tree] itself clings to the rocks and, as much as [it extends] with [its] top to the ethereal breezes, so much with [its] root does it extend into Tartarus. Hardly otherwise the hero is struck with unceasing words from this side and that, and he feels deeply the cares in [his] great heart; his mind remains unmoved, [and] useless tears roll down [lit., are rolled].

AENEID 4.642–705

4.642–705

But Dido, trembling and wild from [her] monstrous undertakings, rolling [her] bloody line of vision, and her trembling cheeks suffused with spots [lit., suffused with respect to her trembling cheeks with spots] and pale with the death about to be [i.e., to come], bursts into the inner thresholds of the house and, crazed, mounts the lofty pyre[s] and unsheathes the Dardanian sword, a gift not sought for these purposes. Here, after she saw the Ilian robes and the familiar bed, having delayed a bit in [*or* through] tears and thought she both lay on the bed and said [her] final words:

"Relics, sweet, so long as the fates and god allowed, receive this life and release me from these cares. I have lived, and I have finished the course [of life] which Fortune had given [to me], and now a great likeness of me will go beneath the earth. I founded a very renowned city, I saw my city walls [i.e., I saw the walls of my city rise], having avenged [my] husband I exacted punishment[s] from [my] hostile brother—fortunate, alas, too fortunate, if only the Dardanian prows had never touched our shores."

She spoke, and having pressed her face on the bed she says, "We shall die unavenged, but let us die; thus, thus does it please [me] to go beneath the shades. May the cruel Dardanian drink in with his eyes this fire from the deep [sea], and let him carry with him the omens of our death." She had spoken, and [her] companions see her collapsed in the middle of such things by/upon the sword, and the sword foaming with blood and [blood-] spattered hands. Shouting goes to the lofty courtyards; Rumor rushes through the shaken city. The halls roar with lamentations and moaning and female shrieking, the upper air resounds with great wailings, not otherwise than if, with enemies having been let in, all Carthage or ancient Tyre were to fall, and raging flames were to roll through the roofs of men and through [the roofs] of gods. [Her] sister, half-dead, heard and, terrified, with a trembling run she rushes through the midst [of the people in the palace], disfiguring [her] face with

[her] nails and [her] breasts with [her] fists, and calls on the dying one by name:

"Sister, was this that [i.e., was this what you were planning]? Were you seeking me in deceit? [Was it] this [that] this pyre of yours, this [that] the fires and altars were preparing for me? Having been forsaken, what am I to complain of first? Did you, dying, spurn your sister [as] companion? [I wish that] you had called me to these same fates, that the same grief and the same hour had carried [us] both off by the sword. Indeed, did I build [your pyre] with these hands and did I call the ancestral gods with [my] voice, so that, with you having been placed thus, I might be apart [from you], cruel one? You have destroyed yourself and me, sister, and the people and Sidonian fathers and your city. Give [her to me so that] I may wash [her] wounds with water[s] and, if any last breath wanders above [her mouth], that I may collect [it] with [my] mouth."

Having spoken thus, she had passed beyond the high steps, and cradled [her] half-dead sister in [her] bosom, having embraced [her] with a groan, and dried the black blood[s] with [her] robe. That one, having tried to raise [her] heavy eyes, falls back; the wound pierced beneath [her] breast hissed. Lifting herself three times and having leaned on [her] forearm, she raised [herself]; three times she was rolled over on the bed and with wandering eyes sought light in the high heaven and groaned, [light] having been found.

Then all-powerful Juno, having taken pity on [her] lengthy grief and difficult passing[s], sent Iris down from Olympus, to [lit., who would] release the struggling soul and the bound limbs. For since she was dying neither by fate nor by a deserved death, but pitiful[ly] before [her] time and inflamed by sudden passion, Proserpina had not yet taken a blond [lock of] hair from that one's head and had [not yet] doomed [her] [lit., the head (of the person)] to Stygian Orcus. Therefore, Iris, dewy with saffron feathers [and] drawing a thousand various colors through the sky, with the sun facing [her], flies down and stood above [Dido's] head. "Having been ordered [to do so], I take this sacred [lock of hair] for Dis [i.e., Pluto] and I release you from this body of yours": thus she speaks, and she cuts the lock with [her] right [hand], and at the same time all the heat departed and life withdrew into the winds.

AENEID 6.1–211

6.1–41

Thus he speaks, crying, and he gives [free] rein[s] to the fleet and at last glides to the Euboean shores of Cumae. They turn the prows to the sea; then with [its] tenacious hook the anchor made fast the ships, and the curved sterns fringe the shores. The eager band of young men darts out onto the Hesperian shore; some [lit., a part] seek the seeds of flame hidden away in veins of flint, some/others [lit., a part] seize upon the crowded homes of wild beasts, the forests, and show the rivers [that have been] found. But faithful Aeneas seeks the citadels on which lofty Apollo presides, and the secret [places] of the Sibyl to be dreaded from afar, a huge cave, [the Sibyl] whose great mind and spirit the Delian prophet inspires and [to whom] he reveals things to be. Now they come up to the groves of Trivia [i.e., Hecate] and the golden halls.

Daedalus, as the story is, fleeing the Minoan kingdom[s], [and] having dared to entrust himself to swift wings in the sky, floated along an unusual [*or* unused] path to the chilly northern constellations, and finally stood light[ly] above the Chalcidian citadel. Having been restored to these lands, he first consecrated to you, Phoebus, the oarage of wings, and established massive sanctuaries. On the doors [was] the death of Androgeos; then [were depicted] the descendants of Cecrops, ordered to pay [as] the penalty (sorrowful!) the bodies of [their] children by sevens annually; the urn stands [there] [i.e., is depicted on the doors], the lots having been drawn. On the opposite side corresponds the Cnosian land, raised up from on the sea; here is present the savage love for the bull, and Pasiphaë subjected to [*or* by] deceit, and the mixed offspring and double-shaped progeny, the Minotaur, reminders of unspeakable Venus/love; here [is depicted] that famous effort of a house and the insoluble wandering; but Daedalus himself, having pitied the great love of the queen, unraveled the tricks of the dwelling and the confusions, directing blind footsteps with a thread. You also, Icarus, would have had a great part in so great a work, had grief permitted it. Twice he had tried to fashion the fallings/misfortunes in gold, twice [his] paternal hands fell. Indeed, straightaway they would have surveyed everything with [their] eyes, had not Achates, already sent ahead, been present, and at the same time the priestess of Trivia and Phoebus, Deiphobe [daughter] of Glaucus, who says such things to the king: "This time does not seek these sights for itself; now it would be better [lit., it will have been better] to slaughter seven bulls from an untouched herd, [and] so many two-year-old [sheep] chosen according to custom." Having addressed Aeneas with such [words] (and the men do not delay the ordered rituals), the priestess summons the Teucrians into the lofty sanctuaries.

6.42–97

The huge flank of the Euboean cliff [is] hewn into a cave, where a hundred broad entrances lead, a hundred mouths, from which rush so many voices, the responses of the Sibyl. They had arrived [lit., it had been come] to the threshold, when the maiden said, "[It is] time to enquire of the fates. The god [is here]! Look! The god!" To this one [lit., to whom] speaking such things before the entrance[s], [there was] suddenly not [one] countenance, not one hue, [her] tresses did not remain arranged; but her panting breast and wild spirits swell with frenzy, and [she is] greater to be seen and not sounding mortal [i.e., like a mortal], when she has been inspired by the power now closer of a god. "Do you hesitate [to enter] into prayers and vows, Trojan Aeneas?" she says. "Do you hesitate? For the great openings of the awestruck dwelling will not gape beforehand." And having said such things she fell silent. A cold shudder ran through the sturdy bones of [lit., to] the Teucrians, and the king pours forth prayers from [his] deepest heart:

"Phoebus [Apollo], having always pitied the heavy struggles of Troy, you who directed the Dardanian weapons and hands of Paris against the body of the descendant of Aeacus [i.e., Achilles], with you as leader I have entered so many seas skirting great lands, and the peoples of the Massylians secluded deep within [Africa], and the fields stretching to the Syrtes; now at last we have grasped the shores of escaping Italy [*or* the fleeing shores of Italy]. [Only] thus far may Trojan (mis)fortune have followed [us], now it is right for you too to spare the Trojan people, all you gods and goddesses, whom Troy and the great glory of Dardania has opposed. And you, o most holy priestess, fore-knowing of what is to come, grant (I seek kingdoms not unowed to my fates) that the Teucrians settle in Latium, and [their] wandering gods and the disturbed divine powers of Troy. Then I shall found a sanctuary of solid marble to Apollo and Trivia, and festival days by/in [lit., from] the name of Phoebus. And great inner chambers await you, too, in our kingdoms: for here I shall place your lots and the hidden fates uttered for my people, and, kindly one, I shall dedicate chosen men [i.e., as priests]. Just do not entrust [your] verses to the leaves, lest disturbed they fly off, a mockery for the swift winds. I ask [that] you yourself recite [them]." He gave an end of speaking with [his] mouth.

But not yet submissive to [lit., enduring of] Phoebus, the priestess, massive, rages in the cave, if [i.e., in the hope that] she might be able to have shaken the great god from [her] breast; so much the more that one [i.e., Apollo] wearies [her] frenzied mouth, taming [her] fierce heart[s], and he molds [her] by controlling [her]. And now a hundred huge openings of the dwelling lay open of their own accord, and they carry the responses of the prophetess through the breezes: "O [Aeneas], having completed at last the great dangers of the sea (but more grievous [dangers] of land [*or* on land] await [you]), the descendants of Dardanus [i.e., the Trojans] will come into the kingdom[s] of Lavinium (release this care from [your] heart), but they will wish even not to have come. Wars, terrible wars, and the Tiber frothing with much blood I see. Not Simois nor Xanthus nor the Doric [i.e., Greek] camps will have been lacking to you; another Achilles [has] already [been] produced in Latium, himself born from a goddess, too. Nor will Juno, having been added to the Trojans, ever be absent, while you as a suppliant in needy things [i.e., in need] will not have begged what peoples of the Italians or what cities! [i.e., Juno will continue to harass you, although you will have asked all the peoples of Italy for help.] A foreign wife [will be] the cause of such great evil again for the Teucrians [i.e., Trojans], and bridal chambers foreign for a second time. You—do not yield to troubles, but instead go more daring[ly] where your fortune will permit you. The first route of safety, [a thing which] you suppose least, will be revealed from a Greek city."

6.98–155

With such words the Cumaean Sibyl sings dreadful mysteries from the inner sanctuary and bellows in [or from] the cave, wrapping the truth in obscurity [lit., obscure things]: Apollo shakes these reins on her in her rage [lit., raging] and turns goads beneath [her] heart. When the frenzy first departed and the mad mouth[s] rested, the hero Aeneas begins: "O maiden, not any new or unexpected aspect of struggles rises up for me; I have anticipated all things and have gone through [everything] in [my] mind with myself beforehand. I ask one thing: since here is said [to be] the door of the infernal king and the gloomy swamp, Acheron having been poured back [i.e., the swamp created by the overflow of Acheron], let it befall [me] to go to the sight and face[s] of [my] dear father; may you [i.e., please] tell the way and open the sacred entrances. I snatched that one on these shoulders through the flames and a thousand pursuing weapons and rescued [him] from the midst of the enemy; that one, having attended my journey, endured all the seas and all the threats of sea and sky with me, [though] feeble [and] beyond [his] strength and the lot of old age. Indeed, the same man, entreating [me], gave me orders to seek you out [as] a suppliant and approach your threshold[s]. Kindly one, I pray, take pity on both son and father (for you are able [to do] all things, and Hecate did not set you to oversee the Avernal groves in vain), if Orpheus was able to summon the shades of [his] wife, relying on the Thracian lyre and [its] tuneful strings, if Pollux redeemed [his] brother with alternating death, and goes and returns [on] the way so often. Why [should I recall] Theseus, [why] should I recall the great descendant of Alceus [i.e., Hercules]? To me [i.e., mine], too, is descent from greatest Jupiter."

With such words he was praying and was holding the altars, when the prophetess began to speak thus: "Trojan descendant of Anchises, begotten from the blood of the gods, the descent to Avernus [is] easy. Nights and days the door of black Dis [i.e., Pluto] lies open; but to retrace [one's] step and escape to the air[s] above, this [is] the task, this is the effort. A few people, whom impartial Jupiter loved or blazing valor carried up to heaven, having been born from the gods, were able [to do this]. Forests hold the middle of all, and Cocytus, gliding in a black bay, encircles [it]. But if [there is] such great love in the [i.e., your] mind, if there is such great desire to swim in the Stygian lakes twice, twice to look upon black Tartarus, and it pleases [you] to indulge in a mad task, receive [the things] which must be accomplished first. A branch, golden in respect to both leaves and flexible twig, lies hidden in/on a dark tree. [It is] said [to be] sacred to [the] Juno of the underworld [i.e., Proserpina]; the whole grove covers this, and the shadows enclose [it] with dark valleys. But it is not granted to enter the hidden places [lit., things] of earth before/until someone has [lit., will have] plucked the golden-haired young from the tree. Beautiful Proserpina ordained that this, her gift, be borne to her. This first one having been torn off [i.e., when this first has been plucked], another gold [branch] is not lacking, and the twig sprouts with similar metal. Therefore, search on high with [your] eyes and pluck by hand [the branch] [having been] found in the proper way. For it itself will follow willing[ly] and easy [i.e., easily], if the fates call you; otherwise, not with any strength [will you be able] to overcome [it] nor will you be able to tear off [the branch] with hard iron. Furthermore, the lifeless body of a friend to you lies (alas, you do not know) and pollutes the entire fleet with death, while you seek oracles and tarry on our threshold. Before[hand], bring this one back to his proper place[s] and bury [him] in a tomb. Bring black animals; let these be the first expiations [i.e., offerings in expiation]. Thus at last you will look upon the groves of Styx and the kingdoms pathless to the living." She spoke, and became silent, [her] mouth having been pressed [i.e., with her mouth closed].

6.156–211

Leaving the cave, Aeneas proceeds with a mournful face, having cast down [his] eyes [lit., having been cast down with respect to his eyes], and he turns over in [his] mind with himself the dark events. To him [lit., to whom] loyal Achates goes [as] a companion and he plants [his] steps with equal cares. They were discussing [lit., joining] many things between themselves in varied conversation, [discussing] which lifeless friend, which body to be buried the prophetess was telling [to them]. And as they came, those men see Misenus on the dry shore, destroyed by an undeserved death, Misenus descendant of Aeolus, than whom no other [was] more excellent to arouse men with bronze [i.e., the trumpet] and to kindle Mars [i.e., war] with song. This one had been a companion of great Hector, around Hector he entered battles, distinguished in both trumpet and spear. After Achilles [as] victor [had] despoiled that one [i.e., Hector] of life, the very brave hero had added himself to Trojan Aeneas [as] an ally, having followed things not inferior. But then, while he by chance makes the seas resound with a hollow conch shell, foolish, and he calls the gods into contests by song, jealous Triton, if it is worthy to believe, had drowned the man, having been caught, in the frothy wave, among the rocks. Then all lamented around [him] with a great uproar, especially faithful Aeneas. Then, [and there is] hardly a delay, weeping they hasten [to accomplish] the commands of the Sibyl, and vie to heap up the altar of the tomb with trees and raise [it or them] to the sky. They go [lit., it is gone] into an ancient wood, the lofty lairs of wild beasts; the pitch-pines fall, the holm-oak resounds having been struck by axes, and the ashen timbers and easily split oak are [lit., is] split by wedges, [and] they roll the huge ash-trees from the mountains.

And Aeneas, the first man among such tasks, encourages [his] companions and is girded with matched weapons. And with his sad heart he himself turns over these things, looking at the boundless forest, and by chance he prays thus: "If [only] now that golden bough in the tree would show itself to us in so great a grove! Since everything—alas!—too truly the prophetess said about you, Misenus." Hardly had he said these things when by chance twin doves came, flying from heaven under [i.e., before] the face[s] itself of the man, and sat on the green ground. Then the very great hero recognizes the maternal birds and happy [i.e., happily] prays: "O, if there is any way, be leaders and direct your course through the breezes into the groves where the rich branch shades the fertile soil. And you, o goddess parent, do not fail [me] in doubtful things [i.e., in an uncertain situation]." Having spoken thus he pressed [his] steps, observing what signs they bear, where they proceed to head. Feeding, they advanced by flying only as much as the eyes of those following by means of keen sight could keep [them in sight]. Thereupon, when they came to the jaws of foul-smelling Avernus, the swift [birds] raise themselves up and, having glided through the liquid air, sit above the twin tree on [their] chosen seats, from where different-colored air of gold shone through the branches. Just as in the woods in wintry cold the mistletoe is accustomed to flourish with new leaf, [the mistletoe] which its own tree does not bear, and [is accustomed] to surround the smooth trunks with yellow offspring, such was the appearance of leafy gold in the shady holm-oak, [and] thus in the light breeze the foil was rustling. Aeneas snatches [it] at once and eager[ly] breaks [it] off, as it clings [lit., delaying], and he carries it beneath the halls of the prophetess Sibyl.

AENEID 6.450–76

6.450–76

Among these [women] [lit., among whom] was wandering the Phoenician Dido, fresh from [her] wounding, in the great wood; as the Trojan hero first stood near her [lit., whom] and recognized [her] dim[ly] through the shadows, like the moon a person sees, or thinks he has seen, rising through the clouds at the beginning of the month, he released tears and addressed [her] with sweet love:

"Unhappy Dido, true, then, [was] the message [which] had come to me that [you] had been destroyed and had pursued the ultimate things [i.e., death] by means of a sword? Was I, alas, the cause of death to you? I swear by the stars, by the ones above and if there is any trustworthiness beneath the deep earth, unwilling[ly], queen, I departed from your shore. But the commands of the gods, which now compel [me] to go through these shades, through places rough with neglect and the deep night, drove [me] with their orders; nor was I able to believe that I was bringing this so great grief to you by [my] departure. Stay your step and do not withdraw yourself from our [i.e., my] gaze. Whom do you flee? This is the last [word] which, by/because of fate, I address to you."

Aeneas was attempting with such words to soothe [her] mind, burning and watching [him] grimly, and was stirring up tears. That one, turned away, was holding her eyes fixed on the ground, and is not moved in expression more by the conversation begun than if hard flint or Marpesian rock stood [there]. Finally she took herself off and, hostile, fled back into the shade-bearing grove, where [her] former husband Sychaeus responds to that one in cares and matches [his] love [i.e., to hers]. Aeneas, nonetheless, struck by [her] harsh misfortune, pursues [her] with tears from afar and pities [her] going [i.e., as she goes].

AENEID 6.847–901

6.847–901

"Others will hammer out more gently breathing bronzes [i.e., sculptures]—I believe so, truly—will draw living expressions from marble, will plead cases better, and will map [better] with the compass the movements of the heavens and will tell of the rising stars [i.e., constellations]; you, Roman, remember to rule the nations with authority (these will be your arts), and to impose rule on peace, to spare the vanquished and to bring down the proud in war."

So [spoke] father Anchises, and he adds these [words] for the ones marvelling: "Look how Marcellus proceeds, outstanding with the *spolia opima* [i.e., a technical term for a certain category of spoils], and how [as] victor he surpasses all men. This man of equestrian rank will steady the Roman state when the great crowd is disturbing [it] [lit., the great crowd being in an uproar], will lay low the Phoenicians [i.e., Carthaginians] and the insurgent Gaul, and will hang up for Father Quirinus the third [set of] weapons won."

And here Aeneas [said] (for he saw going along a young man outstanding in beauty and with shining weapons, but [whose] brow [was] too little cheerful and eyes of/in a gloomy expression): "Who, father, [is] that one, who thus accompanies the man going [i.e., as he goes]? A son, or someone from the great lineage of descendants? What an uproar of companions about! What great impressiveness [or presence] in the man himself! But black night flies about [his] head with a sorrowful shade."

Then father Anchises, tears having sprung up, began: "O son, do not enquire into the great grief of your people; the fates will only show this man to the earth, and will not permit [him] to exist further. The Roman stock [would have] seemed too powerful to you, [gods] above, if these gifts had been secure. How many groans of men will that field [of Mars] bring to the great city of Mars! Or what funerals/deaths will you see, Tiber, when you [will] glide by the fresh[ly-made] burial mound! Neither will any boy from the Ilian [i.e., Trojan] people raise up [his] grandfathers so high [lit., into so much] with [his] promise, nor will the land of Romulus ever vaunt itself so much in any child [it has nursed]. Alas! [what] loyalty, alas! [what] old-fashioned trustworthiness, and right [hand] unvanquished in war! No one would have gone up against that one with impunity, face-to-face against him armed, either when he went as a foot soldier against the enemy or dug the sides of a foaming horse with spurs. Alas, boy to be pitied! If you were in any way to break the harsh fates—! You will [i.e., must] be Marcellus. With full hands, give lilies for me to [or let me] sprinkle purple flowers and heap up the soul of the descendant with these gifts at least, and let me perform the empty ritual." So they roam here and there in the whole region, in the broad fields of mist, and survey everything. After Anchises conducted his son through each and every one of these [lit., which] things and inflamed [his] mind with a love of the coming fame, thereupon he recalls the wars which must be waged next by the man, and he explains [about] the Laurentian peoples and the city of Latinus, and in what way he must avoid or endure [lit., both avoid and endure] each burden.

There are twin doors of Sleep, one of which is said [to be] of horn, by which an easy exit is given to true shades, the other, shining, [is] made from gleaming ivory, but the souls of the dead send false dreams to the heavens. With these words then Anchises there escorts [his] son and the Sibyl together, and sends [them] out by the ivory gate, [and] that one [i.e., Aeneas] cuts a path to the ships and sees [his] comrades again. Then he carries himself by [i.e., along] a straight course to the port of Caieta. The anchor is thrown from the prow; the sterns stand on the shore.

AENEID 10.420–509

10.420–38

Pallas aims for him [i.e., Halaesus], having prayed thus first: "Father Tiber, grant now to this weapon, which I am balancing ready to throw, good luck and a path through the breast of hard Halaesus. Your oak will receive these arms and spoils of the man." The god heard those words; while Halaesus protected Imaon, the doomed man [i.e., Halaesus] offers his breast, unprotected, to the Arcadian weapon.

But Lausus, a great part of the war, does not desert the ranks, terrified by the [so] great slaughter of the man; first he slays Abas who opposed him, the knot and stay of battle. Arcadia's offspring is laid low, laid low are the Etruscans, and you, O Trojans, your bodies [previously] unharmed by the Greeks. The lines of battle clash, their leaders and strength well matched; those in the rear pack the ranks, and the crowding does not allow hands and weapons to move. Pallas presses and pushes on one side, on the other, Lausus [presses] in opposition; nor is there much difference in age [between them], outstanding [as they are] in beauty, but Fortune had denied them a return to their homeland. The ruler of great Olympus did not permit them, however, to clash with each other; their fates await them presently at the hands of a greater enemy.

10.439–73

Meanwhile, his loving sister advises Turnus, who cuts the middle of the battle line with fleet chariot, to come to Lausus' aid. As he saw his allies, [he said]: "It is time to stop fighting; I am borne alone against Pallas, Pallas is owed to me alone; I wish his father himself were present as spectator." He spoke, and his allies withdrew from the plain as was ordered. And at the withdrawal of the Rutulians, the young man [Pallas] looks in amazement upon Turnus, marvelling at his haughty commands, and casts his eyes over [Turnus'] huge body and surveys everything from afar with his fierce gaze. And with the following words he goes against the words of the tyrant: "I shall be praised either for the supreme spoils that [will] have already been captured or for my noble death; my father is equal to either fate. Stop your threats." Having spoken, he proceeds into the middle of the plain; the blood runs cold into the hearts of the Arcadians. Turnus jumped down from his two-horsed chariot, and prepares to enter [combat] on foot and hand to hand. And just as a lion flies [i.e., to his prey] when from a lofty lookout he has seen [sees] a bull standing far off in a field and practicing for battle, not at all different is the appearance of Turnus as he approaches. When he believed that this man would be in reach of a cast spear, Pallas went forward, if [i.e., in the hope that] some luck may help one who is daring although he is not of equal strength, and he speaks thus to the great heaven: "By the hospitality and tables of my father [i.e., by the hospitality of my father's table], which you approached as a guest, I pray to you, Alcides, be present for this huge undertaking. Let him see me take his bloody weapons from him when he is half-dead, and let the dying eyes of Turnus behold me as victor."

Alcides heard the youth, and suppresses a huge groan deep in his heart, and pours forth empty tears. Then the father addresses his son with kind words: "One's day is determined for each person, and for all people the span of life is brief and not to be retraced; but to extend [one's] fame by deeds, this is the task of courage. Under the lofty walls of Troy so many sons of gods fell; indeed, Sarpedon, my son, fell with [them]. His own fates are calling Turnus, too, and he has reached the turning point of the lifetime allotted to him." Thus he spoke, and he turned his eyes away from the fields of the Rutulians.

10.474–89

Then with great strength Pallas sends forth his spear and pulls the shining sword from its hollow scabbard. Flying, it strikes where the uppermost coverings of the shoulder rise up; and pushing its way through the rim of the shield, it finally even grazed [part] of the huge body of Turnus. At this point, Turnus, balancing for a while [in his hand] the wooden spear tipped with sharp iron, throws it at Pallas, and speaks in the following way: "Look [and see] whether my weapon is more able to pierce." He had spoken; and with a vibrating blow the spear-point pierces the middle of the shield, so many layers of iron, so many of bronze, which the encircling hide of a bull surrounds as many times, and it punctures the barrier of his cuirass and his huge chest. That one [i.e., Pallas] pulls the hot weapon from the wound in vain; by one and the same path his blood and his life follow. He falls onto his wound; his weapons resounded above, and as he dies he seeks the hostile earth with his bloody mouth.

10.490–509

Standing close to him, Turnus [spoke] from above: "Arcadians," he said, "remembering my words carry them back to Evander: I send back Pallas as he deserved him. Whatever the honor of a tomb is, whatever the consolation of burial is, I bestow it. His hospitality to Aeneas will hardly cost him a little." And having said such things he pressed the lifeless [Pallas] with his left foot, taking the huge weight of the baldric and the crime impressed [upon it]: in one wedding night, the band of youths slaughtered foully and the bloody bedchambers, which Clonus son of Eurytus had engraved with much gold. Turnus now gloats at this spoil and rejoices having acquired it. [How] ignorant of fate and of future luck is the mind of mortals, [how ignorant] of how to observe moderation when raised up by favorable things! There will be a time for Turnus, when he will wish [will have wished] that Pallas had been bought at great price unharmed, and when he will hate [will have hated] these spoils and the day [itself]. But crowding together, with much groaning and tears, his allies carry back Pallas [having been] placed on a shield. Oh, great grief and glory about to return to your father!—this [is the] first day [that] gave you to war, this same day carries you off, although you leave behind huge heaps of Rutulians.

AENEID 12.791–842

12.791–806

Meanwhile, the king of all-powerful Olympus addresses Juno as she watches the battles from a tawny cloud: "What end will there be now, wife? What, in short, remains? You yourself know and admit that you know that as a native deity Aeneas is owed to the heavens and is borne by the fates to the stars. What are you contriving? Or with what hope do you sit fast in the cold clouds? Was it right that a divinity be injured by a mortal's wound? Or that the sword that had been taken from Turnus be returned to him (for what could Juturna have done without you?), and that strength grow in the ones defeated? Now stop at last and be influenced by my prayers, lest [so] great sorrow eat at you in your silence, and lest sad cares come persistently to me from your sweet mouth. We have arrived at the final hour. You have been able to disturb the Trojans on land and at sea, to kindle an unspeakable war, to disfigure a house and to throw a wedding into confusion with grief; I forbid you to try further."

12.806–28

Thus began Jupiter; thus [spoke] the Saturnian goddess in response, her face [having been] lowered: "Since that will of yours, great Jupiter, is indeed well known to me, I have left, though I am unwilling, both Turnus and the earth. Nor would you see me [i.e., otherwise] alone in this lofty dwelling, suffering things [both] deserved [and] undeserved, but surrounded by flames I would stand at the line of battle itself and would draw the Trojans into hostile battles. I persuaded Juturna—I admit it—to give aid to her poor brother, and I recommended that she dare great things on behalf of his life, but not that she aim the spear, not that she draw tight the bow. I swear [this] by the source of the Stygian spring that is not to be placated, the one source of awe that is given to the gods above. And now I withdraw indeed, and I abandon the battles, detesting [them]. That one thing that is controlled by no law of fate I beseech you, on behalf of Latium and on behalf of the greatness of your descendants: presently when they arrange a peace with auspicious marriage-agreements (so let it be), and presently when they join together laws and treaties, please do not order the native Latins to change their old name, nor to become Trojans and be called Teucri, or the men to change their speech or alter their dress. Let Latium exist, let the Alban kings exist through the ages, let Roman posterity be powerful thanks to Italian excellence. Troy has fallen, and allow it to have fallen, along with its name."

12.829–42

Smiling at her, the creator of mortals and gods [spoke]: "You are the sister of Jupiter and the second child of Saturn, so great [are] the waves of anger you roll beneath your heart. But come now and let go of the wrath undertaken in vain; I grant the thing that you wish, and both overcome [by you] and willing I hand myself over. The Ausonians will keep their ancestral language and customs, and their name will be as it is now; the Trojans will give way, having been mingled [i.e., with the Latins] in body only. I shall add the custom and rites of worship, and shall make all the Latins of one language. The group mixed with Ausonian blood that will rise from here you will see go beyond mortals and beyond gods in religious devotion; nor will any [other] nation celebrate equally the rituals in your honor." Juno nodded to these words and, rejoicing, changed her mind. Meanwhile, she departs from heaven and leaves the cloud.

AENEID 12.887–952

12.887–902

Aeneas presses upon [Turnus] in opposition, and brandishes a huge spear, like a tree; and he speaks thus from his cruel heart: "What, then, is your delay now? Or why do you pull back now, Turnus? We must do battle now not at a run but hand to hand, with cruel weapons. Transform yourself into all shapes and bring together whatever [i.e., resources] you can, whether through courage or through skill. Choose to chase the steep stars on wings or to hide yourself shut up in the hollow earth." Shaking his head, he [replied]: "Your fiery words do not frighten me, fierce man; the gods terrify me, and Jupiter [my] enemy." And saying no more, he looks around for [and sees] a huge rock, a huge [and] ancient rock, which by chance lay on the plain, a boundary-stone placed on the farmland so that it might decide a dispute with regard to the fields. Hardly could twice six chosen men support it on their neck, such [are the] bodies of men [that] the earth now brings forth; that hero hurled against his enemy [the rock] snatched up with shaking hand, rising up higher and stirred up by running.

12.903–27

But he recognizes himself neither as he runs, nor as he goes forth, nor as he lifts and moves with his hand the huge rock; his knees give way, [and] his blood, icy from cold, has congealed. Then the man's stone itself, turning through the empty void, neither traversed the entire space nor accomplished its [intended] blow. And just as in sleep, when sluggish quiet has pressed our eyes with night, we seem to want in vain to extend our eager running, and in the middle of our attempts, we fall, unwell; the tongue has no strength, and the familiar resources in the body are not sufficient, and neither word nor speech follows—thus the dire goddess denies success to Turnus, wherever with bravery he sought a way [or with whatever bravery he sought a way]. Then various sensations are tossed in his breast: he looks to the Rutulians and the city, and he hesitates with fear, and he begins to dread that death is imminent, nor does he see where he may escape, nor with what strength he may aim against the enemy, nor [does he see] his chariots anywhere or his charioteer sister.

Aeneas, having obtained with his eyes [i.e., having seen] a [good] chance, brandishes his death-bearing missile at Turnus as this one hesitates, and with his entire body [Aeneas] aims from afar. Never do stones hurled by a war-machine aiming against the walls resound so, nor do such great clashing noises leap forth from a thunderbolt. The spear flies like a black whirlwind, bearing dire destruction, and exposes the edges of the cuirass and the outermost of the circles of the seven-layered shield; hissing, it pierces [through] the middle of his thigh. Struck, huge Turnus falls to the ground, his knees bent double.

12.928–52

The Rutulians rise up with a groan, and the entire mountain resounds around [them], and the deep groves echo his voice far and wide. That one, brought low, [while] extending his eyes and his beseeching right hand as a suppliant, says, "I deserved this, to be sure, and I do not seek to avoid [you]. Take advantage of your lot. If any concern for a wretched parent can touch you, I beg you (for such was your father Anchises to you), pity Daunus' old age and return me, or if you prefer, [return] my body deprived of light [i.e., the light of life] to my people. You have won, and the Ausonians have seen [me] extend my hands in defeat. Lavinia is your bride; do not go further in hatred." Aeneas stood fierce in his arms, moving his eyes, and he restrained his right hand; and now [Turnus'] speech had begun to bend him as he hesitated more and more, when the unlucky baldric appeared high up on [Turnus'] shoulder, and the swordbelt of the youth Pallas with its familiar studs gleamed, [Pallas] whom Turnus had defeated and laid low with a wound, and [whose] enemy insignia [Turnus] now bore on his shoulders. After he drank in with his eyes the reminder of his savage grief, [Pallas'] spoils, inflamed by rage and dreadful in his wrath, that one [said]: "Are you now to be taken from me here, clothed [as you are] in the spoils of my people? Pallas offers you up with this wound, Pallas, and exacts his penalty from your defiled blood." Saying this, the fiery [Aeneas] buries his sword under the breast opposite him; then [Turnus'] limbs are loosened with cold, and with a groan his life flees beneath the shades, despising [its fate].

QUESTIONS FOR DISCUSSION
AND ANALYSIS
BASED ON SELECTIONS FROM THE *AENEID*

I have assembled below a series of questions on the Latin passages in the accompanying textbook. My purpose has been twofold: to provide teachers with a point of departure for class lectures and discussions; and to help students prepare to be tested in essay format on their comprehension and interpretation of the texts under consideration. It should be obvious to all who consult this list that I have by no means exhausted the store of possible questions that could be raised; my goal has been far more modest, i.e., to alert readers of Vergil to the sorts of issues and questions that can help all readers begin to understand his complex poem.

To make consultation of this list of questions as convenient as possible, I have keyed each question to the relevant section of Latin text as subdivided in the accompanying textbook. In some cases, I have included questions which not only look to the selections in this textbook, but also use other episodes in the *Aeneid* as part of their frame of reference. When teachers and students are not acquainted with these other episodes, I urge them to rephrase the question to make it usable for their purposes; but I also hope hereby to remind my readers that the selections treated here are only part of a much greater poem, and that familiarity with the events, themes, and characters of the poem as a whole is fundamental to an informed comprehension of its parts.

Aeneid **Book 1**

1.1–7

1. How do the first three words of Book 1 establish the theme of the *Aeneid* as a whole?

2. In lines 1–3 (*Troiae ... litora*), Vergil's style is marked by hyperbaton, i.e., the marked separation of words which belong together syntactically. What is the effect of this figure of speech here, and how does it enhance the meaning of these lines?

3. In the first seven lines of Book 1, Vergil summarizes Aeneas' journey from Troy to Italy. How do Vergil's word choice, word placement, and use of figures of speech reflect the significance and difficulty of Aeneas' journey?

1.8–11

4. In lines 8–11, Vergil asks the Muse to help him explain the divine wrath that drives Aeneas on. Identify three different Latin words or phrases used by Vergil to characterize this wrath.

5. In line 10, Vergil describes Aeneas as a man of *pietas* for the first of many times in the *Aeneid*. How is this characterization of Aeneas borne out by his behavior in Book 1—or is it?

6. In line 11 (*Tantaene ... irae*), Vergil uses a rhetorical question to conclude his invocation of the Muse. How does this question anticipate the story told in the rest of the poem? Is this question a satisfactory summary of the poem as a whole? Make your case by referring in detail to at least three different episodes in the poem in which the gods' wrath can be seen to play a major role.

1.12–33

7. Identify three distinct features of Carthage as described by Vergil in lines 12–14 (*Urbs ... belli*).

8. In lines 15–18 (*quam ... fovetque*), Vergil describes Juno's fondness for Carthage. List three features characterizing her affection. How do they complement the description provided earlier in lines 12–14?

9. In line 23, Vergil uses the epithet *Saturnia* to identify and to characterize Juno. To what or to whom does this epithet refer? What reason(s) can you suggest to explain Vergil's use of it here?

10. In lines 24–28 (*prima ... honores*), Vergil lists several reasons for Juno's hatred of Troy. Identify at least three of these, citing the Latin words and phrases to support your answer.

11. In line 32, Vergil mentions fate/the fates for the third time since the poem's opening (the earlier references are in lines 2 and 18). Why do you think that Vergil gives this motif such prominence in the opening lines of the *Aeneid*?

12. In line 33, Vergil concludes his summary of the story told in the *Aeneid*. How can this line be seen as a summary of the entire poem? And how does this summary complement that already provided in line 11 above?

1.34–49

13. At 1.34, Vergil focuses in on the Trojans as they sail in the western Mediterranean sea towards Italy. He thus starts the story *in medias res*, an effective strategy for creating tension and excitement. How has the introduction (lines 1–33) paved the way for the first episode? And how does Vergil create tension and excitement in this episode's opening lines (34–36)?

14. Why does Vergil describe Juno's anger as *aeternum vulnus* (36)?

15. How do the opening words of Juno's monologue (*"Mene ... fatis,"* 37–39) contribute to Vergil's characterization of the goddess?

16. In lines 39–48 (*"Quippe ...gero"*), Juno compares her own inability to exact revenge with Minerva's punishment of Ajax. Are the two situations really comparable? Use the text to support your point of view.

17. In lines 46–47 (*"quae... coniunx"*) Juno explains why she feels she deserves respect. What are three of her reasons?

18. Juno ends her speech with a rhetorical question (48–49). What is the implicit answer to her question?

1.50–80

19. In lines 51–57 (*nimborum ... iras*), Vergil describes the kingdom of the

wind-god Aeolus. Identify three figures of speech or rhetorical devices *other than* alliteration/assonance that Vergil uses to enhance the vividness of these lines.

20. How do lines 51–63 characterize Aeolus himself? Is he an absolute monarch, or is his power limited in any way?

21. In lines 69–70 (*"incute ... ponto"*), Juno suggests four ways Aeolus can damage Aeneas' fleet. What are they?

22. Juno offers Aeolus marriage to the nymph Deiopea in return for his help with disturbing Aeneas' ships (72–75). How does Juno ensure the success of her offer?

23. In lines 76–80 (*"Tuus ... potentem"*), Aeolus describes Juno's power in the universe generally and over him in particular. Do you think that his response would please Juno? Give three reasons for your explanation.

24. What is the purpose of Aeolus' emphatic repetition of the word *tu* in lines 78–79?

1.81–123

25. In lines 81–91, Vergil describes the storm created by Aeolus. How does the structure of Vergil's narrative reflect the destructiveness of the storm?

26. In lines 92–94 (*Extemplo ... refert*), Aeneas himself is introduced as a character in the poem and in the storm created by Aeolus. What first impression of his character do these lines create?

27. In lines 94–101 (*"O ... volvit"*), Aeneas laments the fact that he did not die along with the other great Trojan heroes at Troy. In particular, he mentions Hector and Sarpedon, both of whom will be alluded to again in the *Aeneid*. Were the fates of these two men in fact enviable? You may wish to look at the scenes in the *Iliad* in which the deaths of these two heroes are depicted to support your discussion with specific details.

28. Aeneas' first speech in the *Aeneid* (94–101) has sometimes been criticized for its mournful tone, but has also been considered profoundly moving. Do you think that this speech contributes to a positive or negative first impression of our hero?

29. In line 95, Aeneas refers to the good fortune of those Trojans who died

at home and in the sight of their parents (*"ante ora patrum Troiae sub moenibus altis"*). What factor(s) relating to the context for this speech help to make this reference particularly poignant here?

30. In lines 102–117, Vergil returns to a detailed description of the storm and its destructive powers. Locate four figures of speech and rhetorical devices used in this passage that contribute to the violence of the description.

31. Readers have frequently commented on the visual nature of this description (102–17), and have compared it to painted or even filmed narrative. Draw a picture of or otherwise illustrate Vergil's storm in a visual medium. In your opinion, which medium allows for greater detail, the verbal or the visual? Why?

32. In lines 118–19 (*Apparent ... undas*), Vergil offers a brief description of the storm's aftermath. How does the arrangement of words in these lines complement their meaning?

33. In line 119, Vergil echoes the opening words of Book 1 (*arma virum*). What is the effect of this echo?

34. In lines 120–23, Vergil closes the storm scene by focusing in on the damage done to the Trojan ships. How much damage has in fact been done to Aeneas' fleet? How many ships have been destroyed?

1.124–56

35. In lines 124–27, Neptune emerges from the sea and into the poem, so to speak. Define and describe four figures of speech or rhetorical devices used by Vergil to mark the importance of this entrance. What first impression of Neptune is Vergil seeking to achieve?

36. We have already seen in the storm scene the imbalance of power between Juno and Aeolus, as well as its consequences. With the appearance of Neptune on the scene in line 125, the divine hierarchy is further complicated. How is Neptune related to Juno and Aeolus? And how is his relationship to them likely to affect the divine balance of power?

37. In line 130, Vergil uses the words *doli ... Iunonis et irae* to describe Neptune's perception of the storm and its causes. Is his sense of Juno's motivation justified? What is its basis?

38. In lines 132–41 (*"Tantane ... regnet"*), Neptune addresses the winds

who have caused so much trouble for the Trojans, and reasserts his control over them. What features of structure, style, and word choice make this a particularly effective speech?

39. In line 135 (*"Quos ego—"*), we find the most famous example of aposiopesis in all of Latin literature. Can you think of any particularly striking instances of this device in English?

40. In lines 142–47 (*Sic ... undas*), Vergil describes how Neptune and his attendants restore peace at sea. How does this passage reflect in its style the speed and ease with which Neptune acts?

41. In 148–53 (*Ac ... mulcet*), Vergil uses the first extended simile in the *Aeneid* to describe the effect of Neptune's calming powers on the chaos around him. How do the features of the simile correspond to details in the storm narrative?

42. In this simile, Vergil describes a man of outstanding *pietas* (151) who by the power of his presence is able to calm those around him. While it is clear that Vergil intends in the first place to compare Neptune with this man, his use of the word *pietas* also makes it likely that he means us to think of Aeneas himself. Why might Vergil wish us to see Neptune and Aeneas as similar?

43. With lines 154–56, Vergil closes the storm scene. How do these lines provide an effective ending for this episode, and a transition to the next?

1.157–207

44. With the ecphrasis of the cave of the Nymphs in lines 159–69, Vergil again presents his reader with a striking example of visual narrative. Identify five figures of speech/rhetorical devices Vergil uses to create this vivid picture.

45. The cave of the Nymphs is perceived by the Trojans as a safe harbor where they may rest and recover from the effects of the storm. Is their perception accurate? How does Vergil make the cave seem inviting and safe? And is it so in fact?

46. In lines 170–79 (*Huc ... saxo*), Vergil describes in detail the landing of the Trojans on the Libyan shore and their first actions there. How does Vergil use the contrast between wet and dry states to emphasize this transition?

47. In lines 180–94 (*Aeneas ... omnes*), Vergil depicts Aeneas' first actions upon arriving on the Libyan shore. How does this scene contribute to our evaluation of Aeneas' abilities as a leader?

48. In line 197, Vergil describes Aeneas as soothing his men with his words (*dictis ... mulcet*). This expression has already been used once in Book 1— where? And what parallel does this repetition suggest?

49. In lines 198–207, Aeneas delivers his second speech in the *Aeneid* (the first appears at lines 94–102). Compare the contents of the two speeches as well as their respective audiences. How does the second speech modify your evaluation of Aeneas' character? Or does it?

50. Evaluate the effectiveness of Aeneas' speech. If you were one of his men, would you be reassured? Why?

1.208–22

51. In lines 208–9 (*Talia ... dolorem*), Vergil provides some insight into Aeneas' thoughts. Does this insight have any effect on your evaluation of the preceding speech? Why?

52. In lines 210–22, Vergil describes at length the Trojans' first meal and their subsequent conversation about their lost comrades. How does this scene contribute to the characterization of Aeneas' followers?

1.223–96

53. In lines 223–26 (*Et ... regnis*), Jupiter is introduced into the poem. How do these lines serve to characterize him? Is the first impression created a positive or a negative one?

54. The introduction of Jupiter in the preceding four lines is followed by that of Venus in lines 227–29. How sympathetic is this first impression of Venus? Compare Vergil's description of her to that of Jupiter—what, other than the length of the descriptions, distinguishes them?

55. Much as in Juno's case, Venus' first speech (1.229–53) is essentially a complaint; yet while Venus turns to Jupiter for help, Juno does not. How can the differing approaches of the two goddesses be explained?

56. In lines 231–41 (*"quid ... laborum?"*), Venus describes both the past and present sufferings of her son Aeneas and his followers. To what particular

events is she referring? Cite the appropriate Latin words and phrases to support your answer.

57. In line 237, Venus makes a point of referring to Jupiter as *genitor*. Given the context in which this epithet appears, what might Venus' purpose be in using it here?

58. In line 251, Venus makes her only reference to Juno in this speech (*"unius ob iram"*), suppressing explicit mention of the other goddess's name. What reasons might Venus have for avoiding mention of Juno?

59. In line 252, Venus uses the verbs *prodimur* and *disiungimur* to describe the difficulties plaguing Aeneas' attempt to reach Italy. Why does she use the first person plural here, rather than the third person?

60. In lines 254–56 (*Olli ... natae*), Vergil continues to develop his characterization of Jupiter. How do the details provided here complement the picture already provided in lines 223–26?

61. In his speech to Venus (lines 257–96), Jupiter offers a detailed description of the future that awaits Aeneas and his descendants in Italy. Citing the appropriate Latin words and phrases from this speech, list at least ten future events promised by Jupiter.

62. In his speech, Jupiter establishes an etymological link between the Greek name for Troy, Ilium, and the names of several Roman leaders who are to descend from Aeneas. Locate three stages in Jupiter's prophecy in which this etymological link plays a role.

63. In lines 286–88 (*"Nascetur ... Iulo"*), Jupiter refers to a man named Julius Caesar, whose birth and ascent to power will embody, according to Jupiter, the fulfillment of Roman destiny. This reference has remained controversial for two millennia—does Vergil wish us to think of C. Julius Caesar dictator here, or of his adoptive son Octavian Augustus, whose full name (*tria nomina*) after adoption was also C. Iulius Caesar? To approach this question, you will find it helpful to keep in mind the dates during which Vergil was writing and the major events leading up to the fall of the Roman republic and the ascent of Octavian to sole authority (*princeps*).

64. Jupiter concludes his prophetic speech (lines 291–96) with a description of the eventual achievement of peace under the Caesar named in the preceding lines. He uses several personifications (e.g., Fides) to represent this achievement. Why might he have chosen to use this rhetorical device? And

what is its effect upon Vergil's reader?

1.297–304

65. In this brief transitional passage from the conversation of the gods to the action on earth, Mercury descends from Olympus to prepare Dido for the arrival of the Trojans. Think about the context in which this scene appears, looking both at what precedes and at what follows. Why do you think Vergil thought it important to introduce this transitional scene? What information and/or tone does it add to the narrative that might otherwise be missing?

1.305–417

66. In line 305, we are once again reminded by Vergil of Aeneas' *pietas*. What relevance does this positive quality have in its surroundings—i.e., why does Vergil use the epithet *pius* here?

67. In lines 310–12 (*Classem ... occulit*), Vergil describes the safe harbor in which Aeneas' ships are concealed. How do the word choice and word placement of these lines complement the scene depicted in them?

68. In lines 314–20, Vergil describes in detail Venus' epiphany to her son Aeneas: she is disguised as a maiden out in the woods for a hunt. Is this disguise appropriate to Venus' character? Provide three reasons based on the Latin text here to support your answer.

69. Vergil makes a point of being specific in his description of Venus' disguise—she is like a Spartan or Thracian huntress. What is it about these two ethnic groups in particular that helps to explain Vergil's choice?

70. Venus' speech in lines 321–24 (*"Heus ... prementem"*) is forthright and bold; what figures of speech/rhetorical devices in this speech help to capture this tone?

71. In lines 326–29 (*"Nulla ... una"*), Aeneas begins his response to Venus by challenging her self-identification as a mortal girl. Rather than suspecting her of being his mother, however, he surmises that she may be Apollo's sister Diana or one of the nymphs. Why are these the first guesses Aeneas makes?

72. After reasserting the authenticity of her disguise, Venus proceeds to offer Aeneas a description of the land at which he and his companions have arrived, and to introduce its ruler Dido into the narrative. What about Venus'

first reference to Dido (*"Imperium ... fugiens,"* 340–41) is likely to have captured Aeneas' sympathy from the outset of the queen's story?

73. In lines 343–52, Venus briefly tells of the hostilities between Sychaeus and Pygmalion. How much information does the goddess provide about the character of each of these men? Cite the Latin text to support your answer.

74. In lines 353–56, Venus reports that the ghost of Sychaeus informed Dido of his fate. Although Venus does not explicitly report Dido's reaction to this apparition, how does she evoke Aeneas' sympathy for Dido in these lines?

75. In lines 357–64 (*"Tum ... facti"*), we hear how Sychaeus urged Dido to leave her Phoenician home immediately, and her subsequent preparations. What figures of speech/rhetorical devices does Venus use in these lines to emphasize the sense of urgency expressed by Sychaeus and Dido's response to it?

76. Venus concludes her speech (369–70) by asking Aeneas three specific questions regarding his presence in Carthage. Does Aeneas provide direct answers to her questions? Locate the answer to each of Venus' three questions in the speech of Aeneas that follows.

77. In lines 370–71 (*Quaerenti ... vocem*) Vergil describes Aeneas as *suspirans imoque trahens a pectore vocem*. Why? What do these details contribute to Vergil's portrayal of Aeneas?

78. With the first word of his speech (*"Dea,"* 372), Aeneas asserts his conviction that he is speaking with a goddess. Is there anything about Venus' speech that might have confirmed this suspicion for him?

79. Before beginning their respective stories, both Venus and Aeneas alert their listener(s) to the length and complexity of the story to follow. Compare Aeneas' opening lines at 372–74 with Venus' words at 341–42, and describe the effect of this rhetorical strategy upon its audience.

80. In line 378, Aeneas identifies himself as *pius*. Why does he do so in this context? And how does he himself seem to define the word?

81. In line 379, Aeneas asserts that his fame has already traveled around the world. What basis does he have for making this claim at this point in the story?

82. In lines 381–85 (*"Bis ... pulsus"*), Aeneas summarizes his experiences

in journeying from Troy to Carthage. How does he attempt to evoke sympathy for himself in these lines? And are they consistent with everything he has told Venus previously?

83. In the opening of her response (387–91), Venus instructs Aeneas to find Dido and announces the imminent recovery of his lost ships. How do the word order and word placement in these lines enhance their meaning?

84. After giving Aeneas these instructions, Venus adds a disclaimer to her words: *"Ni frustra augurium vani docuere parentes,"* 392. Why does Venus feel it necessary to say this at this point in her speech?

85. Venus uses the word *augurium* to describe the ability she has to interpret omens (392). This word in its original meaning has to do with the interpretation of the movements and patterns of birds in the sky. Why is this term particularly appropriate here?

86. In lines 393–400, Venus gives a vivid description of the movements of two groups of swans in the sky. What figures of speech/rhetorical devices does she use to increase the vividness of this description? Locate and describe the effect of at least three of them.

87. In lines 402–5 (*Dixit ... dea*), Venus at last reveals her true identity. List three features that prove her divinity here.

88. In 407–9 (*"Quid ... voces"*), Aeneas reproaches Venus as she flees for not having revealed herself to him immediately, and accuses her of having tricked him. Has she in fact done so?

89. In lines 411–14, Vergil describes how Venus conceals her son and Achates in a cloud to protect them as they enter Carthage. What four things does she hope to protect them from?

90. Before moving on to the next scene in Carthage, Vergil closes this episode with three lines describing Venus' destination (415–17). What is the effect of these lines on your interpretation of the preceding scene? And how do they enhance your understanding of the character of Venus?

1.418–40

91. As Aeneas and Achates approach Carthage, they are awed by what they see (lines 418–22). Identify at least four remarkable features of the new city as described here by Vergil.

92. In lines 423–29 (*Instant ... futuris*), Vergil gives a vivid description of the various activities in which the Carthaginians are engaged. Identify at least eight of these activities, and consider the sequence in which Vergil lists them: what does the arrangement suggest about the relative importance of each of these activities?

93. In lines 430–36 (*Qualis ... mella*), Vergil uses a simile comparing the Carthaginian laborers to bees, and notes several of the activities in which bees are typically engaged. How effective is the parallel suggested by this simile? Can you detect any differences between the way in which Vergil describes the Carthaginians and the way in which he describes the bees?

94. Walls (*moenia*, 437) are an important symbol in Roman tradition (and in classical thought generally) of stability, permanence, and civilization; they are also useful for the exclusion of foreigners and defense against enemies. Which of these meanings do the Carthaginian walls have for Aeneas? And which of these meanings do the Carthaginian walls have for the Carthaginians themselves?

1.441–93

95. In lines 441–45 (*Lucus ... gentem*), Vergil describes the grove to which the Phoenicians had come previously and where they had received an omen from Juno confirming this as their new home. A similar sequence of events is described in Book 7, when the Trojans finally arrive on the Italian shores. Compare the omens received by each of these groups. In your opinion, which of these omens is more favorable? And why?

96. What reasons can you think of to help explain Dido's devotion to Juno?

97. The elaborate description of Dido's temple to Juno in lines 448–49 is noted for its difficult syntax—what exactly is Vergil describing? And how does the difficulty of the syntax reflect the construction being described? You may wish to try to draw the scene described by Vergil to help you visualize it.

98. Vergil's triple emphasis on bronze in 448–49 indicates the richness with which Dido's temple was decorated. What other connotations, i.e., besides richness, does bronze have in ancient thought? You may wish to investigate the symbolism of bronze in classical myth to help you with this question.

99. In lines 450–52, Vergil describes Aeneas' new optimism upon seeing Dido's temple of Juno. Upon what beliefs is his optimism based? And what

does this passage contribute to your understanding of Aeneas' character?

100. In lines 456–58, Vergil provides a brief summary of what Aeneas sees depicted on the temple of Juno (*videt ... Achillem*). What is Aeneas' relationship to the three entities singled out here, the Atridae, Priam, and Achilles? Why do you think that Aeneas notices them first? And why does Vergil mention them in the order he does?

101. In lines 459–63, Aeneas encourages Achates to interpret the scenes depicted on the temple in a positive light, because they prove how famous the Trojan war (as well as their role in it) is by now. How long a time has in fact passed between the end of the war and the Trojans' arrival at Carthage?

102. In line 464, Vergil describes Aeneas' study of the scenes on the temple with the words *pictura pascit inani*. How many different translations of this expression can you think of? And how does the translation you prefer affect your interpretation of this scene?

103. The images that make up this *pictura* (464) are depicted somewhere on the temple of Juno—but where? Does Vergil provide any explicit information regarding their placement? If so, what is it?

104. Lines 466–493 contain the ecphrasis of the scenes depicted on the temple of Juno. What words and phrases does Vergil use to suggest the visual nature of his description?

105. How many individual scenes does this ecphrasis contain? And in what order do they appear? Why does Vergil arrange them in this order? And does Vergil suggest that any scene is more important than the others, and if so, how?

106. Why do you think that Dido has chosen to decorate her new temple for Juno with scenes from the Trojan war—i.e., what significance do you think this event has for Dido?

107. Although the ecphrasis of the scenes on Juno's temple is first and foremost an attempt to capture a visual image in words, Vergil also invests this ecphrasis with a great deal of emotion. Make a list of the words and phrases used by Vergil here to express feelings rather than appearances.

108. Vergil does not tell us how Aeneas feels when he sees himself among the characters depicted on the temple (*se ... Achivis*, 488). Basing your argument on what you have already learned about Aeneas' character in Book 1,

what do you think his reaction is likely to have been? And why is it not noted explicitly here?

1.494–519

109. The arrival of Dido on the scene in lines 494–97 (*Haec ... caterva*) brings the ecphrasis to an abrupt end. Does Vergil give any indication that the last scene he describes (lines 491–93) is in fact the last scene on the temple, or is Aeneas poised to look further?

110. In lines 498–502, Vergil compares Dido to the goddess Diana. A Diana-look-alike has already appeared once in Book 1—where? And what does the repetition of imagery associated with Diana suggest about Dido?

111. Vergil's simile here is modeled on a Homeric simile, used to describe Odysseus' reaction when he first sees the princess Nausicaa on Phaeacia after he has been washed ashore there. Read this episode in *Odyssey* Book 6, and compare Vergil's simile to Homer's. How is Vergil's different? And why might Vergil have wanted to introduce such variations?

112. Scenes involving hunting and hunting imagery appear repeatedly in Book 1. Identify three episodes seen so far in which hunting or hunting imagery plays a major role, and discuss the effect of Vergil's repeated use of this motif.

113. In her earlier description of queen Dido, Venus had used the phrase *"dux femina facti"* (364). How does Dido's leadership manifest itself in this scene as Aeneas watches her? Identify three distinct features in the description of Dido in lines 494–519 which support Venus' description.

Aeneid **Book 2**

2.1–56

1. The first word of Aeneas' speech (*"Infandum,"* 3) is ironic, given the etymology of the word. Can you explain its irony in this context?

2. With the opening of his speech (3–9), Aeneas suggests that the story of Troy's fall is in fact too long to be told in one sitting. What is the effect of this rhetorical device?

3. Line 9 (*"praecipitant ... somnos"*) is a notable example of onomatopoeia. Why do you think Aeneas uses this figure of speech here?

4. In his description of the building of the Trojan horse (11–20), Aeneas begins to use verbs in the present tense although the events described took place many years earlier. What reason(s) might Aeneas have for using the present tense? And what is its effect on the story he tells?

5. In lines 26–30 (*"Ergo ... solebant"*), Aeneas describes the rejoicing of the Trojans at the apparent departure of the Greeks. Identify at least 4 activities mentioned in these lines that the Trojans can now take pleasure in.

6. In lines 30–31, Aeneas uses the verbs *"stupet"* and *"mirantur"* to describe the reaction of the Trojans to the wooden horse. Where else in the *Aeneid* have you seen a reaction to something new described in these terms?

7. In lines 35–38 (*"At ... latebras"*), Aeneas describes the various suggestions made to dispose of the horse. Identify at least three of these with specific reference to the Latin text.

8. With what verb is the noun *latebra* (38) cognate? And why is its use particularly appropriate here?

9. How is the meaning of line 39 reflected in its word order?

10. One of the first words used by Aeneas to describe the priest Laocoon is *ardens* (41). What is its meaning here?

11. In lines 42–49 (" *'O ... ferentes'* ") Laocoon addresses the people of Troy. Is this a rhetorically compelling speech? Support your answer with reference to the text.

12. In lines 50–53 (*"Sic ... cavernae"*), Aeneas describes the hurling of Laocoon's spear and its impact. Identify three figures of speech/rhetorical devices used by Aeneas to make this a particularly vivid and emotional description.

13. In lines 54–56, Aeneas uses a so-called mixed condition, combining both tenses of the subjunctive (imperfect and pluperfect) used in contrary-to-fact conditions as well as the pluperfect indicative *impulerat*. Explain the logic underlying Aeneas' choice of tenses and moods here.

2.199–227

1. In line 200, Laocoon is identified as a priest of Neptune. Why does Vergil include this information here? Do you think it has any relevance to Laocoon's fate?

2. In lines 203–4, Vergil separates the epithet *gemini* far apart from the word it modifies, *angues*. What is the effect of this separation (hyperbaton) on Aeneas' audience?

3. In line 209, the clause *"Fit sonitus spumante salo"* is virtually impersonal, i.e., no hearer is specified. What effect does this sort of description have on its audience? And how do other features of these words enhance this effect?

4. Aeneas focuses particular attention in his description of the snakes on how their eyes look, i.e., *"ardentes ... oculos suffecti sanguine et igni"* (210). How literally are we to take this description? Support your answer with reference to the text.

5. Aeneas describes the movement of the snakes toward Laocoon with a military metaphor, *agmine certo* (212). Why do you think Aeneas uses this metaphor?

6. The description of the snakes' assault in lines 213–19 (*"et ... altis"*) uses language associated with several of the five senses (i.e., sight, taste, smell, hearing, and touch). Find an example in this passage of at least one word or phrase associated with three of these senses, and describe the effect of this appeal to the senses on Aeneas' audience.

7. The scene of the snakes' attack on Laocoon and his sons as described by Aeneas is often compared to the famous Laocoon sculpture depicted on p. 77. Which representation of the story do you prefer, and why?

8. Do you think that Vergil was familiar with the Laocoon sculpture when he composed this scene? Use Vergil's text as the basis for your argument.

9. What is the rhetorical purpose of Aeneas' uses of tmesis, or the cutting of one word into two parts (*circum ... dati*), in lines 218–19?

10. In lines 223–24 (*"qualis ... securim"*), Aeneas uses a simile to compare the bellowing of Laocoon to that of a bull in the process of being slaughtered. Why do you think Aeneas chooses to use this simile in particular, i.e., what does it tell us about Laocoon and his suffering?

11.After wreaking their destruction the snakes depart swiftly and smoothly (lines 225–27). Why do you think Vergil focuses on the nature of their departure to end this scene?

2.228–67

12. In lines 228–33 (*"Tum ... conclamant"*), Aeneas offers an ironic summary of the effect of Laocoon's suffering upon the other Trojans. Identify at least three ironic details in this passage.

13. Some scholars think that lines like 235 here are incomplete because Vergil did not finish the *Aeneid* before he died. Can you think of any other explanation for the incomplete line that is relevant to the story Aeneas is telling?

14. In lines 234–40 (*"Dividimus ... urbi"*), Aeneas describes the actions taken by the Trojans as they receive the horse into the city. Identify three separate actions mentioned by Aeneas here.

15. How difficult must it have been to move the horse into the city? Use the description given in lines 234–40 to support your answer.

16. Identify three figures of speech/rhetorical devices used by Aeneas in lines 241–42 (*"O ... Dardanidum"*) to communicate his strong emotion.

17. In line 245, Aeneas refers to the horse as a *monstrum infelix*. How do the etymologies of both of these words (*monstrum* from *moneo*, 'warn,' and *infelix* from *fero*, 'bear' or 'be fertile') help to explain Aeneas' choice of words?

18. In lines 250–53 (*"Vertitur ... artus"*), Aeneas uses 4 separate clauses to describe the arrival of night and the sleep of the Trojans. The scene is super-

ficially a peaceful one, but a few ominous features are present in Aeneas' language. Can you find three ominous details in this passage?

19. In line 255, Aeneas mentions the island Tenedos, behind which the Greek fleet was hiding. Why does he make a point of referring to it here?

20. In lines 259–64, Aeneas provides a list of names of the Greeks released from the horse by Sinon. How many are there? And what figures of speech/rhetorical devices does Aeneas use in this passage to create variety and make the list memorable?

21. In line 265, Aeneas describes Troy as *"urbem somno vinoque sepultam,"* although it is the people in the city and not the city itself who are drunk and sleeping. Why do you think Aeneas chooses to describe the scene this way?

22. In lines 266–67, Aeneas lists four things done by the men in the horse upon their release. What are they?

2.268–97

23. In line 269, Aeneas describes sleep as a gift of the gods (*"dono divum"*). Given what we have already learned about gifts in Book 2, what are the implications of this expression here?

24. In lines 270–73, Aeneas describes the appearance of Hector at the time of his death. How did Hector die?

25. In lines 274–76, Aeneas recalls two of Hector's greatest accomplishments as described in the *Iliad*. What are they?

26. In describing the conversation he had with Hector in his dream, Aeneas uses the verb *videbar* of himself (line 279). Why? What is the effect of this verb here?

27. In lines 281–86, Aeneas quotes the speech he delivered to Hector's ghost in his sleep. What figures of speech/rhetorical devices does he use in this speech to express his emotional state?

28. Hector's response in lines 289–95 (*" 'Heu ... ponto' "*) is straightforward and clear. Identify at least four things Hector tells Aeneas to do.

29. Throughout this scene, Vergil has used language relating to hiding and concealment to describe the fall of Troy. Identify at least five different words

Vergil uses that are in some way associated with this motif. What is the effect of the repetition of this motif on Vergil's reader?

2.469–525

1. The name of Achilles' son Pyrrhus is etymologically connected with the Greek word for fire, *pyr*. How does Vergil take advantage of this connection in lines 469–75?

2. In the simile of lines 471–75, Pyrrhus is compared to a snake that has shed its old skin. How does the snake imagery used here complement that which appears earlier in Book 2? How is it different?

3. In lines 479–82 (*"Ipse ... fenestram"*), Aeneas describes Pyrrhus' violent assault on the palace of Priam. How does Aeneas' word choice contribute to the violent tone of the description?

4. In lines 483–85 (*"Apparet ... primo"*), the interior of the palace is described. What figures of speech/rhetorical devices does Aeneas use in these lines to enhance the sense of foreboding they provoke?

5. Aeneas' description of what is going on further inside the palace (486–88) is in strong contrast with the three preceding lines. What makes the contrast so striking?

6. Aeneas emphasizes the fear of the women in the palace by describing their frenzied activity in lines 489–90. Identify three of their actions.

7. In lines 491–95 (*"Fit ... complent"*), Pyrrhus and the other Greeks break into the palace at last. How do Aeneas' word choice, word placement, and use of the hexameter complement the violence he describes?

8. In the simile of lines 496–99 (*"Non ... trahit"*), Pyrrhus and his followers are compared to a raging river. What elements in the simile are meant to parallel the palace of Priam and the people within it? And how do these parallels add to the poignancy of the scene?

9. Aeneas reminds of his presence as a witness to the preceding scene with his reference to himself in 499: *"Vidi ipse ...."* How does the placement of these words in the line contribute to their impact?

10. Pyrrhus has two names: the second, Neoptolemus, appears in line 500. The etymology of this name is Greek, too, from 'new' (*neo*) and 'war'

(ptolemos). Why do you think that Vergil might have wanted to introduce the second name into this scene?

11. In line 506, Aeneas addresses Dido directly (*"requiras"*) and reminds us that she is his primary audience. Why does Aeneas think that Dido will be particularly interested in the fate of Priam?

12. In lines 507–11, Aeneas provides a poignant description of Priam's final attempts to defend himself and his home. What features in Aeneas' description help to evoke our sympathy for Priam?

13. At the center of Priam's palace, according to Aeneas, there are an altar and a laurel tree (512–14, *"Aedibus ... penates"*). Why does Aeneas provide this information? What does it contribute to the story?

14. In lines 515–17, Hecuba and her daughters are compared to a flock of doves. What associations do doves have in classical thought? Find at least two, and consider their relevance to the scene shown here.

15. In her attempt to make Priam put down his arms, Hecuba tells him that his help is useless now: *"non, si ipse meus nunc adforet Hector"* (522). What exactly does she mean?

2.526–66

16. The death of Priam's son Polites in lines 526–32 serves briefly to postpone the death of Priam. Aeneas could have chosen to tell this story more quickly, or to include Polites among the members of Priam's household already described. Why do you think that Aeneas (or Vergil) might have wanted to single out Polites here? And what is the effect of this episode on the surrounding narrative?

17. In composing Priam's final address to Pyrrhus (535–42), Vergil suggests a fundamental comparison between father and son. The relationship of fathers and sons has been developed as an important theme on several other occasions in Book 2; choose one of these examples and discuss the similarities between that scene and this one.

18. In lines 541–43 (*" 'sed ... remisit' "*) Priam describes three actions performed by Achilles when they met. What were these actions? And what do they tell us about the character of Achilles?

19. Aeneas uses lines 544–46 to illustrate how weak and defenseless Priam

is. Which words and phrases in this passage serve to evoke our pity for Priam?

20. Pyrrhus' response (" '*Referes* ... *morere,*' " 547–50) is sarcastic and surprisingly short. How do the contents of his speech and its brevity contribute to his portrayal in the *Aeneid*? Are they consistent with what has been seem of him previously?

21. After Aeneas describes the death of Priam, he pauses to reflect on its symbolism (554–58), equating the death of Priam with the fall of Troy. How does Aeneas use Priam's corpse to symbolize Troy?

22. After the death of Priam, Aeneas is suddenly reminded of his own father, his home, and his family (559–66). Vergil thus uses the father-son theme as a link to the next scene; how do Aeneas' thoughts of his home, wife, and son also support this link?

23. In line 560, Aeneas describes his sudden recollection of his father as the apparition of an *imago*, a word often used to describe the appearance of a dead person in one's dreams. Is Aeneas' father already dead? How can you tell?

2.735–67

1. In lines 735–36, Aeneas attributes his confusion to the interference of *"nescio quod ... male numen amicum."* Why is Aeneas so vague about the divinity's identity here? And who are the most likely candidates for this description?

2. Aeneas' confusion continues as he describes his loss of his wife Creusa in lines 736–40 (*"Namque ... nostris"*). What are the two possible explanations he gives for this loss?

3. Aeneas reports that he did not realize his loss until he and his fellow exiles reached a place sacred to Ceres (*"tumulum antiquae Cereris sedemque sacratam,"* 742). Who is the goddess Ceres? What does she have in common with Aeneas that may help to explain his reference to her here?

4. Aeneas asks a rhetorical question in line 745: *"Quem non incusavi amens hominumque deorumque ...?"* Can you think of one important person he appears to have forgotten to blame?

5. In lines 752–59 Aeneas recalls what he saw when he re-entered Troy in

search of Creusa. Is he describing events during the day or the night? How can you tell?

6. Aeneas' next stop is the palace of Priam (760–67). What does he see there? And how does this description recall his earlier description of the palace in lines 483–95?

2.768–804

7. In lines 772–73, Aeneas uses three different nouns to describe the apparition of Creusa that appears before him. What are these three words? What is the difference between and among them? And what does Aeneas' use of three similar terms rather than one suggest about his emotional state?

8. In line 780, Creusa uses an odd metaphor to describe sailing: *"'vastum maris aequor arandum.'"* What kind of activity is normally implied by *arandum*? Why does she use it here? And is the resulting image a positive or negative one?

9. In lines 780–84, the shade of Creusa prophesizes to Aeneas his safe arrival in Hesperia. Identify at least five positive facets of Creusa's prophecy, citing the Latin text in support of your answer.

10. In lines 790–94, Aeneas describes his vain attempts to hold onto the shade of Creusa. This moving passage is made even more memorable by Aeneas' use of numerous figures of speech/rhetorical devices. Identify at least three of these, and explain what they contribute to the deep emotion expressed in this passage.

11. Aeneas' heroism has been thought by some scholars to be compromised by his (at best) careless loss of Creusa in Book 2. Do you think he could have prevented this loss? Do you think this event reflects on his character in either positive or negative terms? Refer to details in the Latin text of Book 2 to support your answer.

12. What effect is Aeneas' story of his loss of Creusa likely to have on Dido?

13. With the close of Book 2, Aeneas brings the story of the fall of Troy to an end, describing in lines 796–804 his departure from Troy accompanied by a small band of fellow exiles. Identify at least three details of this conclusion that make this an effective ending for the book. What sort of emotional or psychological effect is this ending likely to have had on Aeneas' Carthaginian audience?

Aeneid **Book 4**

4.1–53

1. In lines 1–5, Vergil vividly portrays Dido's emotional turmoil as she recognizes her love for Aeneas. Identify at least three figures of speech used by Vergil in these lines to describe Dido's feelings.

2. In lines 9–29, Dido speaks to her sister Anna about her inner turmoil. Discuss how Vergil uses the structure of Dido's speech to reinforce its contents.

3. In lines 10–14, Dido provides a list of the things that make Aeneas attractive to her. Identify five of them.

4. In lines 24–27, Dido prays for terrible things to happen to her if she violates her vow to Sychaeus. Compare this prayer with the scene in Book 6 in which Aeneas meets Dido in the underworld (lines 450–76). How closely does her present wish match her eventual fate?

5. In her response (lines 31–53) Anna tries to dissuade Dido from remaining faithful to her vow. How successful is she? And why?

6. In this speech (lines 31–53) Aeneas offers Dido a number of reasons why a union of some sort with Aeneas would not be a bad thing, both for Dido herself and for her people. Identify four different reasons given by Anna, citing the Latin text in support of your answer.

7. In lines 35–38 (*"aegram ... amori?"*), Anna refers to the many suitors Dido has already rejected. The motif of a queen rejecting many suitors is one which Vergil's readers would have recognized as being based on a somewhat similar situation in the *Odyssey*. Who are the parallels to Aeneas and Dido in Homer's poem? How comparable is their situation to that represented here? And what do you think is the most important difference between the two couples?

4.54–89

8. In lines 56–64, Vergil describes the rituals performed by Dido in hopes of arousing a mutual desire for her in Aeneas. Identify three different activities pertaining to these rituals. Are these typical of rituals described in the *Aeneid* or not?

9. In lines 58–59, Vergil names the four divinities to whom Dido makes offerings. Why does she attend to these gods in particular? What does she expect each of them to be able to do for her?

10. Juno is identified as the most important of the divinities to whom Dido makes offerings, because she presides over marriage. Can you think of any other special association(s) which might make Juno a favorite goddess of Dido's?

11. In lines 66–69 (*Est ... furens*), Vergil uses fire imagery to describe the passion consuming Dido. How is this imagery complemented by the word placement in these lines?

12. In lines 69–74 (*qualis ... harundo*), Vergil compares Dido to a doe mortally wounded by a hunter. Where else have you seen Vergil use hunting imagery? On the basis of these scenes, do you think that Vergil considers hunting a good (i.e., productive) activity, or not?

13. There are many different wild animals to which Vergil could have compared Dido. Why do you think he chooses the deer for this comparison, as opposed to any other animal? What about this animal's nature might have attracted Vergil's interest and sympathy?

14. In lines 74–85, Vergil establishes a contrast of sorts between Dido's infatuated daytime activities and those she engages in at night. Identify at least five different figures of speech/rhetorical devices Vergil uses in these lines to illustrate both the parallels and the contrasts between the two times of day.

15. In lines 86–89, Vergil suggests that the future of Carthage is endangered by Dido's love for Aeneas. According to Vergil, what is the connection between the two, i.e., civic and private affairs?

4.90–128

16. With line 90, Venus moves from narrating events in Carthage to a scene involving the gods. How has he prepared us for this shift in the preceding scene?

17. In line 94, Juno addresses Venus and Cupid as *"tuque puerque tuus."* There is some ambiguity in the words *puer ... tuus*, however—to whom else can they refer? And what are the implications of this alternative for your reading of the passage?

18. In line 94, Juno identifies Cupid parenthetically with the phrase *"magnum et memorabile numen."* Why does she say this? And does she mean it as a compliment?

19. In her reply to Juno (107–14) Venus reveals again that she is a brilliant rhetorician. Identify and describe four features of Venus' speech that help to make it so agreeable to Juno.

20. In her response to Venus (115–27) Juno sets forth her plan to bring Dido and Aeneas together. Identify at least four actions Juno plans to take to ensure their union.

21. In lines 127–28 (*Non ... repertis*) Vergil describes Venus' response to Juno's plan. Does she approve? Why?

4.129–72

22. In lines 129–32, Vergil describes general preparations for the hunt. What figures of speech/rhetorical devices does he use to create excitement and anticipation?

23. In line 133, Vergil describes Dido as *cunctantem*. What explains her delay?

24. How does the word order of line 137 complement what is being described?

25. In this scene, Vergil describes Aeneas as *ante alios pulcherrimus omnes* (141), and then uses a simile to compare him to Apollo (lines 141–50). How does this description/comparison complement that given of Dido in Book 1.496–504?

26. The description given of Ascanius in lines 156–59 makes him seem somewhat older than he had been when he appeared in Book 1. How much time has passed between the two scenes? What other factors can account for Ascanius' relative maturity here?

27. The description of the storm in lines 160–68 is extremely ominous. What figures of speech/rhetorical devices does Vergil use here to increase our sense of foreboding as we read?

28. How sympathetic is Vergil to Dido? Use his comments in lines 169–72 as the basis for your answer.

4.173–218

29. Vergil's description of Fama (lines 173–88) creates a terrifying personification of an abstract force. Besides personification, what figures of speech/rhetorical devices does Vergil use to explain Fama's power?

30. Scan line 181. How does the metrical pattern of the line complement its meaning?

31. In line 188, Vergil indicates that Fama reports both true and false rumors. Is there anything untrue about the rumors she spreads in lines 191–94?

32. Compare the ritual activities of Iarbas here (lines 198–202) with those of Dido in lines 56–64. How similar are their goals?

33. Iarbas' speech to Jupiter betrays his wounded pride, much as had Juno's speech betrayed hers in Book 1.37–49. Compare these two speeches: what structural features and rhetorical devices do they have in common?

34. In lines 215–17, Iarbas uses several cultural stereotypes to insult Aeneas and his men. Does Vergil provide any indication in the remainder of the *Aeneid* that these stereotypes may have a basis in truth?

4.219–95

35. In lines 223–37, Jupiter tells Mercury to remind Aeneas of his purpose and destiny. How would you characterize the tone of Jupiter's speech—is he worried, or angry, or annoyed, or unemotional about the current state of affairs? Cite the specific language used by Vergil to support your answer.

36. Is Jupiter aware of the plotting of Juno and Venus? How do you know?

37. In the detailed description of lines 238–44 Vergil describes Mercury's preparations for travel to earth. Using only the information provided by Vergil, draw a picture of Mercury as he is depicted here.

38. In lines 242–44, Vergil describes Mercury's wand (*virga*). How many different things can the god do with this instrument? List them. What do they all have in common?

39. In his description of Atlas (lines 246–51), Vergil depicts the Titan as both god and mountain simultaneously. Identify at least four figures of speech/rhetorical devices Vergil uses here that contribute to Atlas' duality.

40. In lines 253–55 (*hinc ... iuxta*), Vergil compares Mercury to a bird flying at sea. How does this simile contribute to Vergil's characterization of Mercury?

41. In lines 260–64, Vergil describes Aeneas as Mercury sees him when he arrives in Carthage. What are we supposed to think of Aeneas' appearance? And how does his appearance complement the activities in which he is engaged?

42. In lines 266–76 (*"Tu ... debetur"*), Mercury addresses Aeneas and gives him Jupiter's message. How closely does Mercury's speech represent what Jupiter had told him to say? And how similar is the tone of Mercury's speech to that of Jupiter?

43. Vergil describes Aeneas' reaction to Mercury's speech as a combination of shock and terror (279–80). What features of Mercury's speech and presentation are likely to have added to Aeneas' dread?

44. In lines 281–86, Vergil vividly depicts Aeneas' inner turmoil. What figures of speech/rhetorical devices does Vergil use in this passage to help us understand Aeneas' emotional state of mind?

45. In lines 288–94, Vergil lists the things Aeneas decides to do. How many activities are included? List them, and discuss the effect of listing them in the order provided by Vergil.

4.296–330

46. In lines 300–303, Dido is compared to a frenzied Bacchant as she hears the rumors about Aeneas' impending departure. Does this simile arouse sympathy for her in Vergil's reader? Support your response with reference to the Latin text.

47. In her speech to Aeneas (305–30), Dido moves from anger to sarcasm, from reproach to desperation. Discuss the range of emotions reflected in her speech, and evaluate the speech's general persuasiveness.

48. In lines 307–8, Dido speaks of herself in the third person. What is the intended effect of this rhetorical device?

49. In lines 320–26, Dido mentions a number of political reasons for her not to want to lose Aeneas. Some of the same reasons have been used elsewhere in Book 4 to convince Dido that a marriage to Aeneas would be advanta-

geous. Where are these earlier discussions of political expedience? And are they consistent with what Dido says here?

50. Dido's wish for a *parvulus ... Aeneas* (328–29) evokes the theme of the role of children in the continuity of the family and the survival of the Trojans. Where else has this theme been developed in Book 4, and by whom?

4.331–92

51. In lines 336–61, Aeneas defends himself to Dido. Is this a convincing speech of self-defense? Does it allow us to feel sympathy for Aeneas' point of view? Use specific features of Aeneas' speech to make your case.

52. In lines 337–39 (*"Neque ... veni"*), Aeneas claims never to have misled Dido, either about their relationship or about his departure. Is this true? Support your answer with reference to specific details in the narrative of Aeneas' stay in Carthage.

53. In lines 351–59, Aeneas mentions the three characters who have had the greatest effect on his decision to leave. Who are they? And which one of these do you think has the greatest power over Aeneas? Why?

54. Aeneas' words in line 361, *"Italiam non sponte sequor,"* are perhaps his most famous; yet they remain ambiguous. What do you think Aeneas means, exactly? And why does he say this at the close of his speech to Dido?

55. Lines 362–64 describe a short pause before Dido responds. Before she speaks, does Vergil give any clue in these lines to her reaction to what Aeneas has said?

56. Dido's response in lines 365–87 is filled with passion and anger, and ends in a curse. Although it is highly emotional, however, it is also carefully planned and assembled by Vergil. Discuss how Vergil uses the structure of the speech, and details like word choice, word placement, and figures of speech/rhetorical devices, to characterize the forcefulness of Dido's response.

57. In lines 388–92, Vergil closes this dramatic scene with a final glimpse of each of the two main characters. How has each of them reacted to each other's speech(es)? Does Vergil leave his reader feeling equal sympathy for both of his characters, or does he suggest greater sympathy for one over the other? Explain your answer with reference to the text.

58. How does Vergil use word choice and word placement in lines 393–96 to illustrate Aeneas' divided emotions?

59. In lines 401–7, Vergil compares the bustling Trojans to hard-working ants gathering food and bringing it home. Identify four ways in which the Trojans' behavior is comparable to that of the ants. And how does it differ?

60. In line 408, Vergil takes the remarkable step of addressing Dido directly. What effect does this intrusion have upon the narrative, and upon Vergil's depiction of Dido?

61. In line 410, Vergil changes his addressee to Amor. How can you explain the poet's continued involvement of himself in this scene?

62. In lines 413–15, Vergil lists the things Dido does in a last desperate attempt to make Aeneas change his mind. How can we tell beforehand that she is likely to be unsuccessful? Refer to the Latin text to support your answer.

63. In her speech to Anna (lines 416–36), Dido once again displays her rhetorical skills and so deceives her sister. How much of her speech is the truth? How much is falsehood? And how does Dido use irony and double meanings to her advantage?

64. In lines 438–49, Vergil compares Aeneas to a sturdy oak that has the ability to resist all the winds by which it is buffeted. Under some circumstances, this simile might well be used to reinforce a very positive portrayal of Aeneas—can you think of such a situation in the parts of the *Aeneid* you have already read? Do you think that in this context Vergil intends us to read this simile as a positive affirmation of Aeneas' heroism, or does he use it to show Aeneas' limits? Use the details in the Latin text to support your answer.

65. In lines 441–46, what figures of speech/rhetorical devices does Vergil use to illustrate the steadiness of the oak and the violence of the winds?

4.642–705

1. The description of Dido's behavior in lines 642–50 is filled with action. How many separate activities does Dido engage in in these lines? And what is the impression of her mental state created by all of this activity?

2.In lines 651–62, Dido delivers her final speech. How would you characterize this final speech—vengeful, pitiful, overly emotional, or manipulative? Or something other than these? Use the details of the Latin text to support your discussion.

3. Fama appears for the last time in Book 4 at line 666. Consider how her presence permeates Book 4, discussing at least three different scenes in which Fama/fama is featured. Why is she of such great thematic significance in this book and in the *Aeneid* generally?

4. In lines 675–85 (*"Hoc ... legam"*), Anna expresses her astonishment at Dido's sudden suicide. Should she be surprised? Is there any way she could have anticipated Dido's intentions? Use her speech to support your discussion.

5. In lines 688–92, Vergil describes Dido's dying actions. Why does he include this scene? It would have been possible for him not to include it; what effect do you think he is striving to achieve with it?

6. Juno appears in lines 693–95, and sends down Iris to release Dido from life. Why doesn't Juno go herself? Can you think of a parallel to this use of a divine intermediary that occurs elsewhere in Book 4?

7. Dido's departure from life coincides with the end of the book. Is this a satisfying conclusion, or do important questions raised in the book remain unanswered? Use the text to support your discussion.

Aeneid **Book 6**

6.1–41

1. In lines 1–8, what epithets does Vergil use to capture the eagerness of Aeneas' men for their arrival in Italy?

2. The motif of secrecy and hiddenness permeates the opening of Book 6 (lines 1–13). Identify five words or phrases which contribute to this motif.

3. In lines 5–8, Vergil describes the activities of Aeneas' men upon their arrival at Cumae. List three of these activities.

4. Aeneas' first act upon his arrival at Cumae is to head for the shrine of Apollo there (*At ... petit,* 9–11). Why is Aeneas so devoted to Apollo? Describe one other scene in the *Aeneid* in which Aeneas' devotion to Apollo is evident.

5. In lines 14–19, Vergil tells the story of Daedalus' earlier journey to Cumae. How did Daedalus make this journey? Identify three phrases used by Vergil to describe Daedalus' unusual mode of transport.

6. Identify at least two similarities between Aeneas' and Daedalus' arrivals at Cumae as suggested by the wording of lines 14–19.

7. Making two columns on the page to help you visualize what Vergil is describing, identify and list at least three scenes on each of the doors of the temple of Apollo (*In ... manus,* lines 20–33).

8. Would you characterize the decoration on the doors as symmetrically arranged or not? In 2–3 sentences, defend your choice.

9. Who speaks the parenthetical *miserum!* in line 21, Vergil or Aeneas? Explain your choice.

10. The first of the doors is described in three lines (20–22). Identify at least three figures of speech used in these lines, and describe their effect on the reader.

11. Crete (*Cnosia tellus,* 23) was visited by Aeneas and his men in their journey across the Mediterranean. Where does this scene occur? Was their visit there fortunate, or was it a negative experience? Why?

12. Vergil describes the scenes on the second door as *Veneris monimenta nefandae* (26). What exactly does this mean? And does this phrase represent Aeneas' interpretation of the scenes, or Vergil's?

13. In lines 27–30 (*hic ... vestigia*), Vergil describes the labyrinth of the Minotaur without using the word 'labyrinth.' What Latin words and expressions are used instead to evoke the building and its unusual design?

14. The ambiguous reference to a queen (*regina*) in line 28 invites us to think of two famous Cretan queens, Pasiphaë and Ariadne. What aspects of their stories have special relevance to the Trojans looking at these doors?

15. Vergil's subtle allusion to the story of Theseus and Ariadne in lines 28–30 was inspired in part by a lengthy version of the same story told by Catullus in his poem 64. Read this poem in English, and briefly discuss the relevance of Catullus' poem to the story of the *Aeneid*.

16. The word *ambages* (line 29) is, appropriately, ambiguous, and can be used in a variety of different contexts. Can you think of one other scene in the *Aeneid* where this word is used? Compare its meaning there to its meaning in the present scene.

17. In lines 30–33 (*Tu ... manus*) Vergil describes something that is not in fact depicted on the door. Do you think that Aeneas knows this story and is likely to be thinking of it as he views the doors? Or is this information that we have but he does not?

18. The story of Daedalus and Icarus is frequently used in ancient literature to illustrate the close relationship between fathers and sons. This theme is one we have also seen developed in several scenes in the *Aeneid*. What does this scene contribute to our understanding of the relationship as Vergil depicts it?

19. The ecphrasis on the doors of the temple of Apollo has sometimes been interpreted as advice or a warning (cf. the relationship of the words *'monimentum'* and *'moneo'*) to Aeneas and his men. What lesson or warning are they being given? And do you think that they comprehend it?

6.42–97

20. The Sibyl's cave is described in lines 42–44. How well does the description fit the photograph on p. 170?

21. The transformation of the Sibyl (*Cui ... dei*, 46–51) is described in physical terms, but has psychological implications as well. What aspects of Vergil's description suggest that Apollo has affected not only the Sibyl's appearance but also her mind?

22. Aeneas' reaction to the Sibyl's transformation is described as a cold shudder (*Gelidus ... tremor*, 54–55). Locate one other scene in the *Aeneid* in which Aeneas grows cold. Are the experiences similar in any other respect?

23. In the opening of his prayer to Apollo (56–61), Aeneas lists a number of reasons why he has reason to be grateful to the god. List at least four of these reasons.

24. In lines 56–68, Aeneas addresses three different entities. Who are they? And why does he address them in this order?

25. What two things does Aeneas promise to do for Apollo if Apollo grants his prayer now (lines 71–72)? Does Aeneas ever fulfill this vow?

26. In lines 71–76 (*"Te ... oro"*) Aeneas addresses the Sibyl with the vocative *alma*. Why does he call her this?

27. In lines 84–97, the Sibyl prophesizes the arrival of the Trojans at their destined home, but also lists a series of obstacles they have yet to overcome. Identify five of these obstacles. In which books of the *Aeneid* do we see each of them play a major part?

28. In line 89, The Sibyl refers to Turnus as *"alius ... Achilles."* Given what you know about the characters and fates of Turnus and Aeneas, is this parallel appropriate?

29. Prophetic speeches like the Sibyl's are typically intentionally ambiguous or difficult to interpret. Does Aeneas understand how to interpret everything in this speech?

6.98–155

30. In lines 98–102 (*Talibus ... quierunt*), Vergil describes the Sibyl's behavior as if she were an animal while under the influence of Apollo. Find at least three different words or expressions in this passage which contribute to this characterization.

31. With the first words of his response to the Sibyl (*"Non ... peregi,"*

103–5), Aeneas tells her that he is prepared for whatever lies ahead. Why does he say this? Do you believe him?

32. Given Vergil's repeated emphasis on the relationship between father and son, it is perhaps not surprising that he here asks the Sibyl to help him visit Anchises in the underworld. How and where did Anchises die?

33. In lines 110–14, Aeneas describes all that he and his father have been through together. What figures of speech/rhetorical devices does Vergil use in this passage to accentuate the mutual interdependence of father and son?

34. In line 117, Aeneas again addresses the Sibyl as *alma* (cf. line 74 above). Why does he repeat this epithet here?

35. In lines 119–23, Aeneas lists 4 other heroes (or pairs of heroes) who have successfully traveled to the underworld and back, so that the Sibyl will look kindly on his request to do the same. How comparable in fact to Aeneas are these heroes and their missions to the underworld? And what differences make Aeneas' mission unique?

36. What figures of speech/rhetorical devices does Aeneas use in lines 119–23 to make his request as compelling as possible? Find at least three, and describe their likely emotional impact on the Sibyl.

37. In line 126, the Sibyl addresses Aeneas not with the vocative of his name but as *Tros Anchisiade*." What is the significance of her choice of epithets?

38. In lines 129–31 (*"Pauci ... potuere"*) the Sibyl warns Aeneas that only heroes especially beloved by Jupiter have been able to accomplish this journey. Has Aeneas received any indication yet that he might belong to this group? And how does this qualification fit the heroes mentioned earlier, in lines 119–23?

39. In lines 136–44, the Sibyl describes in detail the golden bough that Aeneas will need for a successful journey to the underworld. In particular, she emphasizes the material from which it is made; how many different words and phrases in this passage tell us that it is gold? And why do you think that the material from which it is made should be so important?

40. In lines 142–43 (*"Hoc ... instituit"*), the Sibyl informs Aeneas that the golden bough is to be an offering from him to the goddess Proserpina. Why does this goddess in particular have an interest in this gift? It will be useful for you to investigate how Proserpina got her present position as queen of

the underworld in order to answer this question.

41. In lines 145–48, the Sibyl tells Aeneas the signs by which he will know whether he is destined to pick the bough successfully and make the trip to the underworld. What are three of these signs?

42. In lines 149–53, the Sibyl tells Aeneas that he must first purify himself and his mission by performing a ritual and sacrifice in honor of a dead friend. Who is this friend, and how did he die? And why doesn't Aeneas know about this already?

6.156–211

43. Line 160 describes the conversation between Aeneas and Achates when they leave the Sibyl. Translate this line as literally as possible, being sure to consider a number of meanings for the verb *sero*. Do we have any idioms in English comparable to the Latin expression?

44. In lines 162–74, Vergil briefly summarizes the life and death of Aeneas' comrade Misenus. Make a list of at least five accomplishments for which Misenus is to be remembered.

45. In line 172, Vergil describes Misenus as *demens*. Why?

46. In line 173, Vergil inserts the clause *si credere dignum est* into the story of Misenus' fate. Why does he include this in the story? What features of the story does it draw special attention to?

47. In lines 175–83, Vergil describes how the companions of Misenus attend to his funeral rites. What do these rites consist of? And how do the Trojans show their high esteem for their friend as they conduct these rites?

48. In lines 179–83, the Trojans gather five different types of wood for the pyre. What types are they? And why do you think Vergil mentions so many kinds of wood here—i.e., what is the intended effect on his reader?

49. In lines 190–92 (*Vix ... solo*), two doves suddenly appear on the scene. Where else has Vergil described the sudden appearance of a pair of animals that represent an omen of some sort?

50. In lines 192–97, Aeneas immediately interprets the doves as a good omen sent by his mother. Why does he come to this conclusion so quickly? And how good is Aeneas generally at interpreting omens and other signs?

51. Translate lines 119–200 as literally as possible. What exactly are the doves doing in these lines?

52. In lines 205–9, Vergil uses a simile to compare the leaves on the golden bough to a branch of mistletoe. What is the basis of this comparison? How are these two plants similar, and how do they differ?

53. The description of the bough plucked by Aeneas as *cunctantem* (line 211) is curious. What could explain the bough's slowness to yield to Aeneas' pull?

6.450–76

1. As the word *recens* in line 450 reminds us, Dido's suicide had occurred not long before. Does Vergil provide enough information about the passage of time experienced by the Trojans in Book 5 for us to determine how long it in fact has been? You should read Book 5 in English to help you answer this question.

2. In line 455, Aeneas mentions the *"verus ... nuntius"* which reported her death to him. How would he have received this message? And who might its bearer have been?

3. Is Aeneas' speech (lines 455–66) a compelling self-defense or not? Discuss the rhetorical strengths and weaknesses of this speech. Can you think of anything more Aeneas might have said in his own defense, or any arguments against him that Dido might have used had she chosen to speak in response?

4. Vergil uses imagery associated with darkness and light repeatedly in Book 6 to describe the events in Cumae and in the underworld. Focusing on this scene (450–76), analyze Vergil's use of this imagery. How does it contribute to the characterization of both Dido and Aeneas here?

6.847–901

1. In lines 847–50, Anchises lists the civilized accomplishments to be achieved by people other than the Romans. How many different areas of accomplishment does he mention? And what are they?

2. In line 851, Anchises uses the vocative *"Romane"* to address both Aeneas and, by extension, all of his descendants. This epithet is an anachronism. Why?

3. In lines 851–53, Anchises lists what he believes to be distinctively Roman accomplishments, or *artes*. What are they? Do you think that Vergil's readers at the end of the first century BC would have agreed?

4. In lines 855–59, Anchises describes the elder Marcellus. What figures of speech/rhetorical devices does he use to enhance the vividness of the description? And which of Marcellus' many accomplishments does he seen to think most worth of note?

5. In lines 863–66, Aeneas describes the younger Marcellus. List four features Aeneas notes in his description. What do these four features tell Aeneas about the young man, whom he of course cannot recognize?

6. In his response to Aeneas (lines 868–86), Anchises describes how and why the young Marcellus will be mourned. How many accomplishments of the young Marcellus does he list, and what are they?

7. What sort of funeral does Anchises envision for Marcellus? Compare this imaginary funeral to another funeral depicted in the *Aeneid*. What features do they have in common?

8. The young Marcellus is the last in a long parade of heroes in the underworld as described by Anchises to Aeneas in Book 6. What reasons might Vergil have had for putting him at the end of this parade? And what effect does this placement have on the reader?

9. In lines 888–92, Vergil summarizes the various lessons and instructions given by Anchises to Aeneas to encourage him as he pursues his goal of creating a new home for the Trojans in Italy. Find at least references Vergil makes here to other episodes in the *Aeneid*.

10. In lines 893–99, Vergil describes the two gates from the underworld. Why do you think that Aeneas and the Sibyl depart from the underworld by means of the ivory gate?

Aeneid **Book 10**

10.420–38

1. In lines 420–24, Pallas prays to Father Thybris (Tiber) for success in battle. Why does he pray to this god in particular?

2. In lines 426–30 (*At ... Teucri*), Vergil describes the success of Lausus and his men in the battle. Identify at least three figures of speech used in this passage, and explain their effect on the reader.

3. In lines 433–38 (*Hinc ... hoste*), Vergil foreshadows the deaths of both Pallas and Lausus. What expressions and images in this passage help to convey this foreshadowing?

4. How does Vergil indicate in this passage as a whole for which side in the battle he sympathizes? Or does he?

10.439–73

5. How does Turnus' speech in lines 441–43 (*"Tempus ... adesset"*) contribute to his characterization?

6. Explain the nature of Turnus' wish in line 443. Why does he wish this?

7. In lines 445–47 (*At ... visu*), Vergil describes Pallas' reaction to the sight of Turnus. Why does he have this reaction? Is this reaction consistent with what you already know about Pallas?

8. Why does Pallas refer to his father in his response to Turnus (450)?

9. In lines 454–56 (*At ... imago*), Vergil uses a simile to describe the relationship between Turnus and Pallas in battle. Explain the terms of the comparison. What does this simile contribute to Vergil's depiction of the two heroes' confrontation?

10. In lines 460–63 (*"Per ... Turni"*), Pallas makes a second prayer. To whom does he pray, and why?

11. Beginning with line 464, the scene suddenly shifts from the battlefield to the gods above. How is this shift brought about? What is the effect of this shift in scene on the narrative?

12. In lines 467–72 (*"Stat ... aevi"*), Jupiter offers a brief philosophical statement regarding the nature of heroism. Explain Jupiter's philosophy by specifying at least three of its tenets. What experience has Jupiter himself had that has helped him achieve his wisdom?

13. Throughout this passage (439–73), Vergil emphasizes the relationship between fathers and sons. Identify at least three different sets of fathers and sons mentioned or alluded to in this passage, and explain what Vergil's emphasis contributes to the characterization of these men.

10.474–89

14. In lines 476–78 and 482–85, Vergil depicts the spears of Pallas and Turnus each striking their opponent. How are the two descriptions similar? How do they differ? What figures of speech and other literary devices does Vergil use to characterize the effectiveness of each weapon?

15. In line 489, the earth upon which Pallas falls is described as *hostilis*. Why does Vergil use this epithet?

10.490–509

16. In lines 491–94 (*"Arcades ... largior"*), Turnus makes an offer. What is it? Does his gesture of generosity here cause us to side with Turnus?

17. Identify the scene depicted on Pallas' baldric and described in lines 497–98 (*una ... cruenti*). Why does Vergil characterize this scene as *nefas* (497)? And why is Pallas wearing it?

18. In lines 501–5 (*Nescia ... oderit*), Vergil comments on the ironies of fate, particularly as they are to be experienced shortly by Turnus. Identify three things that, according to Vergil, Turnus will soon come to regret.

19. Vergil closes his description of Pallas' death with a three-line apostrophe (507–9). To whom or to what is this apostrophe addressed? What is the emotional and rhetorical effect on the reader of this conclusion to the scene? Can you compare another instance of Vergil's use of apostrophe with this one?

Aeneid Book 12

12.791–806

1. Throughout his speech (793–806), Jupiter emphasizes the relentlessness of Juno's quest for vengeance against the Trojans. We discover subsequently from Juno's response that Jupiter's speech has been effective. What qualities make it a successful speech? Be sure to look particularly at the structure of the argument and at the rhetorical devices Jupiter uses.

2. To what does Jupiter refer with the words *"Ventum ad supremum est"* (803)?

3. At the end of his speech (lines 803–5: *"Terris ... hymenaeos"*), Jupiter lists a number of Juno's destructive acts against the Trojans. Identify specifically three of the acts to which Jupiter refers here, with reference to the events of the earlier books of the *Aeneid*.

12.806–28

4. Look carefully at the structure and rhetorical artfulness of Juno's response to Jupiter (808–28). How convincing is her speech? How can we be reasonably confident that she means what she says?

5. At line 816, Juno swears an oath by the river Styx. What is the significance of this reference to one of the rivers of the underworld?

6. In lines 821–28 (*"cum ... Troia"*), Juno briefly summarizes the future history of Rome. What are three specific features of this summary? And to what events recorded elsewhere in Roman historical sources do they correspond?

12.829–42

7. Jupiter begins his speech (lines 830–31, *"Es ... fluctus"*) by emphasizing the fact that he and Juno are siblings. Why? How does his description of her in line 831 reflect upon himself?

8. In his speech (830–40), Jupiter gives in to the demands just expressed by Juno (see the previous passage, especially lines 821–29). Compare the two speeches, and discuss how closely his concessions meet her demands. Why is he so willing to go along with her?

9. Jupiter closes his speech (lines 838–40, *"Hinc . . . honores"*) by men-

tioning the positive results to be produced by Juno's reconciliation to the survival of the Trojans in Italy. Looking closely at these lines, explain two reasons for Juno's satisfaction as foreseen by Jupiter.

12.887–902

1. In this passage, Vergil uses the word *ingens* three times; in the first instance (line 888), it is used to describe Aeneas' spear. What is the effect of this word in this description? And what is the effect of its repetition later in the same passage? Can you find any other instances of this word in the remainder of the selection from Book 12? If so, comment on its significance in its new context.

2. In lines 891–93 (*"Verte ... terra"*), Aeneas challenges Turnus to escape him by changing his form. Identify two of the possible different forms Aeneas suggests that Turnus take. What mythological character not otherwise appearing in the *Aeneid* do these transformations suggest?

3. In lines 894–95 (*"Non ... hostis"*), Turnus responds by saying he does not fear Aeneas; he is terrified only by the gods and Jupiter. Why does Turnus single out Jupiter? And why is Jupiter Turnus' enemy?

4. In describing the rock which Turnus picks up to use as a weapon against Aeneas (lines 896–900, *Nec ... tellus*), Vergil mentions that nowadays not even twelve strong men would find it easy to lift this rock. It is clear that this detail is at least in part intended to emphasize the sheer size of the rock; but what other effects does this detail have upon our understanding of the duel between Turnus and Aeneas?

5. Why does Vergil place the word *heros* so emphatically at the end of line 902?

12.903–27

6. Identify the figures of speech and rhetorical devices used by Vergil in his description of Turnus' state (lines 903–5, *Sed ... sanguis*). How do they contribute to the creation of a vivid, and ominous, description?

7. In lines 908–14, Vergil uses a simile to describe the strange physical and emotional symptoms which Turnus experiences in his attempt to escape Aeneas (*Ac ... negat*). What makes this a successful device for helping us to "see" Turnus' condition? And how does the simile contribute to our understanding of the other actions described in this scene?

8. In lines 914–18 (*Tum ... sororem*), Vergil describes Turnus' confusion by listing his different reactions to what is happening around him. List four of these reactions (*sensus*) mentioned by Vergil.

9. In lines 921–23 (*Murali ... crepitus*), Vergil uses another simile, this time to describe Aeneas' assault upon Turnus. To what two things is the force of Aeneas' blow compared? Can you suggest any possible reasons why Vergil has chosen these two items as particularly appropriate for this simile?

12.928–52

10. Lines 928–29 (*Consurgunt... remittunt*) capture the immediate response of his surroundings to Turnus' fall. What three details in particular does Vergil offer us to paint the scene? Can you identify the literary devices, other than alliteration or assonance, which make this description memorable and effective?

11. In his plea for mercy from Aeneas, Turnus mentions Aeneas' dead father, Anchises (line 934). Why?

12. Turnus' basic request in his final speech is that Aeneas return him to his family and people. In lines 935–36 (*"et me ... meis"*), Turnus mentions two possible conditions in which Aeneas may choose to return him: what are they?

13. In line 945, to what do the words *saevi monimenta doloris* refer?

14. As Aeneas prepares to kill Turnus, he not only mentions Pallas as the reason for his action but even makes Pallas the subject of the verbs *immolat* and *sumit* (line 949). Why does reference to Pallas play such a prominent role in this closing scene? Does it help us to see Aeneas' action as a just solution?

15. At the close of the poem, Turnus' soul is said to descend to the underworld *indignata* (952). Why? What does this mean? And can you identify one other character in the *Aeneid* whose death is described in identical terms?

SELECTIONS FROM VERGIL'S *AENEID*

BOOK 1.1–519

Arma virumque cano, Troiae qui primus ab oris

Italiam fato profugus Laviniaque venit

litora, multum ille et terris iactatus et alto

vi superum, saevae memorem Iunonis ob iram,

multa quoque et bello passus, dum conderet urbem   5

inferretque deos Latio; genus unde Latinum

Albanique patres atque altae moenia Romae.

Musa, mihi causas memora, quo numine laeso

quidve dolens regina deum tot volvere casus

insignem pietate virum, tot adire labores   10

impulerit. Tantaene animis caelestibus irae?

Urbs antiqua fuit (Tyrii tenuere coloni)

Karthago, Italiam contra Tiberinaque longe

ostia, dives opum studiisque asperrima belli,

quam Iuno fertur terris magis omnibus unam   15

posthabita coluisse Samo. hic illius arma,

hic currus fuit; hoc regnum dea gentibus esse,

si qua fata sinant, iam tum tenditque fovetque.
Progeniem sed enim Troiano a sanguine duci
20 audierat Tyrias olim quae verteret arces;
hinc populum late regem belloque superbum
venturum excidio Libyae; sic volvere Parcas.
Id metuens veterisque memor Saturnia belli,
prima quod ad Troiam pro caris gesserat Argis—
25 necdum etiam causae irarum saevique dolores
exciderant animo; manet alta mente repostum
iudicium Paridis spretaeque iniuria formae
et genus invisum et rapti Ganymedis honores:
his accensa super iactatos aequore toto
30 Troas, reliquias Danaum atque immitis Achilli,
arcebat longe Latio, multosque per annos
errabant acti fatis maria omnia circum.
Tantae molis erat Romanam condere gentem.
Vix e conspectu Siculae telluris in altum
35 vela dabant laeti et spumas salis aere ruebant,
cum Iuno aeternum servans sub pectore vulnus
haec secum: "Mene incepto desistere victam
nec posse Italia Teucrorum avertere regem!
Quippe vetor fatis. Pallasne exurere classem
40 Argivum atque ipsos potuit summergere ponto
unius ob noxam et furias Aiacis Oilei?

Ipsa Iovis rapidum iaculata e nubibus ignem

disiecitque rates evertitque aequora ventis,

illum exspirantem transfixo pectore flammas

turbine corripuit scopuloque infixit acuto;   45

ast ego, quae divum incedo regina Iovisque

et soror et coniunx, una cum gente tot annos

bella gero. Et quisquam numen Iunonis adorat

praeterea aut supplex aris imponet honorem?"

Talia flammato secum dea corde volutans   50

nimborum in patriam, loca feta furentibus Austris,

Aeoliam venit. hic vasto rex Aeolus antro

luctantes ventos tempestatesque sonoras

imperio premit ac vinclis et carcere frenat.

Illi indignantes magno cum murmure montis   55

circum claustra fremunt; celsa sedet Aeolus arce

sceptra tenens mollitque animos et temperat iras.

ni faciat, maria ac terras caelumque profundum

quippe ferant rapidi secum verrantque per auras;

Sed pater omnipotens speluncis abdidit atris   60

hoc metuens molemque et montes insuper altos

imposuit, regemque dedit qui foedere certo

et premere et laxas sciret dare iussus habenas.

Ad quem tum Iuno supplex his vocibus usa est:

"Aeole (namque tibi divum pater atque hominum rex   65

et mulcere dedit fluctus et tollere vento),

gens inimica mihi Tyrrhenum navigat aequor

Ilium in Italiam portans victosque penates:

incute vim ventis submersasque obrue puppes,

70   aut age diversos et dissice corpora ponto.

Sunt mihi bis septem praestanti corpore Nymphae,

quarum quae forma pulcherrima Deiopea,

conubio iungam stabili propriamque dicabo,

omnes ut tecum meritis pro talibus annos

75   exigat et pulchra faciat te prole parentem."

Aeolus haec contra: "Tuus, O regina, quid optes

explorare labor; mihi iussa capessere fas est.

Tu mihi quodcumque hoc regni, tu sceptra Iovemque

concilias, tu das epulis accumbere divum

80   nimborumque facis tempestatumque potentem."

Haec ubi dicta, cavum conversa cuspide montem

impulit in latus; ac venti velut agmine facto,

qua data porta, ruunt et terras turbine perflant.

Incubuere mari totumque a sedibus imis

85   una Eurusque Notusque ruunt creberque procellis

Africus, et vastos volvunt ad litora fluctus.

Insequitur clamorque virum stridorque rudentum;

eripiunt subito nubes caelumque diemque

Teucrorum ex oculis; ponto nox incubat atra;

intonuere poli et crebris micat ignibus aether 90

praesentemque viris intentant omnia mortem.

Extemplo Aeneae solvuntur frigore membra;

ingemit et duplices tendens ad sidera palmas

talia voce refert: "O terque quaterque beati,

quis ante ora patrum Troiae sub moenibus altis 95

contigit oppetere! O Danaum fortissime gentis

Tydide! Mene Iliacis occumbere campis

non potuisse tuaque animam hanc effundere dextra,

saevus ubi Aeacidae telo iacet Hector, ubi ingens

Sarpedon, ubi tot Simois correpta sub undis 100

scuta virum galeasque et fortia corpora volvit!"

Talia iactanti stridens Aquilone procella

velum adversa ferit, fluctusque ad sidera tollit.

Franguntur remi, tum prora avertit et undis

dat latus, insequitur cumulo praeruptus aquae mons. 105

Hi summo in fluctu pendent; his unda dehiscens

terram inter fluctus aperit, furit aestus harenis.

Tres Notus abreptas in saxa latentia torquet

(saxa vocant Itali mediis quae in fluctibus Aras,

dorsum immane mari summo), tres Eurus ab alto 110

in brevia et syrtes urget, miserabile visu,

inliditque vadis atque aggere cingit harenae.

Unam, quae Lycios fidumque vehebat Oronten,

ipsius ante oculos ingens a vertice pontus

115   in puppim ferit: excutitur pronusque magister

volvitur in caput, ast illam ter fluctus ibidem

torquet agens circum et rapidus vorat aequore vertex.

Apparent rari nantes in gurgite vasto,

arma virum tabulaeque et Troia gaza per undas.

120   Iam validam Ilionei navem, iam fortis Achatae,

et qua vectus Abas, et qua grandaevus Aletes,

vicit hiems; laxis laterum compagibus omnes

accipiunt inimicum imbrem rimisque fatiscunt.

Interea magno misceri murmure pontum

125   emissamque hiemem sensit Neptunus et imis

stagna refusa vadis, graviter commotus, et alto

prospiciens summa placidum caput extulit unda.

Disiectam Aeneae toto videt aequore classem,

fluctibus oppressos Troas caelique ruina;

130   Nec latuere doli fratrem Iunonis et irae.

Eurum ad se Zephyrumque vocat, dehinc talia fatur:

"Tantane vos generis tenuit fiducia vestri?

Iam caelum terramque meo sine numine, venti,

miscere et tantas audetis tollere moles?

135   Quos ego—sed motos praestat componere fluctus.

Post mihi non simili poena commissa luetis.

Maturate fugam regique haec dicite vestro:

non illi imperium pelagi saevumque tridentem,

sed mihi sorte datum. Tenet ille immania saxa,

vestras, Eure, domos; illa se iactet in aula 140

Aeolus et clauso ventorum carcere regnet."

Sic ait, et dicto citius tumida aequora placat

collectasque fugat nubes solemque reducit.

Cymothoe simul et Triton adnixus acuto

detrudunt naves scopulo; levat ipse tridenti 145

et vastas aperit syrtes et temperat aequor

atque rotis summas levibus perlabitur undas.

Ac veluti magno in populo cum saepe coorta est

seditio saevitque animis ignobile vulgus

iamque faces et saxa volant, furor arma ministrat; 150

tum, pietate gravem ac meritis si forte virum quem

conspexere, silent arrectisque auribus astant;

ille regit dictis animos et pectora mulcet:

sic cunctus pelagi cecidit fragor, aequora postquam

prospiciens genitor caeloque invectus aperto 155

flectit equos curruque volans dat lora secundo.

Defessi Aeneadae quae proxima litora cursu

contendunt petere, et Libyae vertuntur ad oras.

Est in secessu longo locus: insula portum

efficit obiectu laterum, quibus omnis ab alto 160

frangitur inque sinus scindit sese unda reductos.

Hinc atque hinc vastae rupes geminique minantur

in caelum scopuli, quorum sub vertice late

aequora tuta silent; tum silvis scaena coruscis

165   desuper, horrentique atrum nemus imminet umbra.

Fronte sub adversa scopulis pendentibus antrum;

intus aquae dulces vivoque sedilia saxo,

Nympharum domus. hic fessas non vincula naves

ulla tenent, unco non alligat ancora morsu.

170   Huc septem Aeneas collectis navibus omni

ex numero subit, ac magno telluris amore

egressi optata potiuntur Troes harena

et sale tabentes artus in litore ponunt.

Ac primum silici scintillam excudit Achates

175   suscepitque ignem foliis atque arida circum

nutrimenta dedit rapuitque in fomite flammam.

Tum Cererem corruptam undis Cerealiaque arma

expediunt fessi rerum, frugesque receptas

et torrere parant flammis et frangere saxo.

180   Aeneas scopulum interea conscendit, et omnem

prospectum late pelago petit, Anthea si quem

iactatum vento videat Phrygiasque biremes

aut Capyn aut celsis in puppibus arma Caici.

Navem in conspectu nullam, tres litore cervos

185   prospicit errantes; hos tota armenta sequuntur

a tergo et longum per valles pascitur agmen.

Constitit hic arcumque manu celeresque sagittas

corripuit fidus quae tela gerebat Achates,

ductoresque ipsos primum capita alta ferentes

cornibus arboreis sternit, tum vulgus et omnem   190

miscet agens telis nemora inter frondea turbam;

nec prius absistit quam septem ingentia victor

corpora fundat humi et numerum cum navibus aequet;

hinc portum petit et socios partitur in omnes.

Vina bonus quae deinde cadis onerarat Acestes   195

litore Trinacrio dederatque abeuntibus heros

dividit, et dictis maerentia pectora mulcet:

"O socii (neque enim ignari sumus ante malorum),

O passi graviora, dabit deus his quoque finem.

Vos et Scyllaeam rabiem penitusque sonantes   200

accestis scopulos, vos et Cyclopia saxa

experti: revocate animos maestumque timorem

mittite; forsan et haec olim meminisse iuvabit.

Per varios casus, per tot discrimina rerum

tendimus in Latium, sedes ubi fata quietas   205

ostendunt; illic fas regna resurgere Troiae.

Durate, et vosmet rebus servate secundis."

Talia voce refert curisque ingentibus aeger

spem vultu simulat, premit altum corde dolorem.

210   Illi se praedae accingunt dapibusque futuris:

tergora diripiunt costis et viscera nudant;

pars in frusta secant veribusque trementia figunt,

litore aena locant alii flammasque ministrant.

Tum victu revocant vires, fusique per herbam

215   implentur veteris Bacchi pinguisque ferinae.

Postquam exempta fames epulis mensaeque remotae,

amissos longo socios sermone requirunt,

spemque metumque inter dubii, seu vivere credant

sive extrema pati nec iam exaudire vocatos.

220   Praecipue pius Aeneas nunc acris Oronti,

nunc Amyci casum gemit et crudelia secum

fata Lyci fortemque Gyan fortemque Cloanthum.

Et iam finis erat, cum Juppiter aethere summo

despiciens mare velivolum terrasque iacentes

225   litoraque et latos populos, sic vertice caeli

constitit et Libyae defixit lumina regnis.

Atque illum tales iactantem pectore curas

tristior et lacrimis oculos suffusa nitentes

adloquitur Venus: "O qui res hominumque deumque

230   aeternis regis imperiis et fulmine terres,

quid meus Aeneas in te committere tantum,

quid Troes potuere, quibus tot funera passis

cunctus ob Italiam terrarum clauditur orbis?

Certe hinc Romanos olim volventibus annis,

hinc fore ductores, revocato a sanguine Teucri, 235

qui mare, qui terras omnes dicione tenerent,

pollicitus—quae te, genitor, sententia vertit?

Hoc equidem occasum Troiae tristesque ruinas

solabar fatis contraria fata rependens;

nunc eadem fortuna viros tot casibus actos 240

insequitur. Quem das finem, rex magne, laborum?

Antenor potuit mediis elapsus Achivis

Illyricos penetrare sinus atque intima tutus

regna Liburnorum et fontem superare Timavi,

unde per ora novem vasto cum murmure montis 245

it mare proruptum et pelago premit arva sonanti.

Hic tamen ille urbem Patavi sedesque locavit

Teucrorum et genti nomen dedit armaque fixit

Troia, nunc placida compostus pace quiescit:

nos, tua progenies, caeli quibus adnuis arcem, 250

navibus (infandum!) amissis unius ob iram

prodimur atque Italis longe disiungimur oris.

Hic pietatis honos? Sic nos in sceptra reponis?”

Olli subridens hominum sator atque deorum

vultu, quo caelum tempestatesque serenat, 255

oscula libavit natae, dehinc talia fatur:

“Parce metu, Cytherea, manent immota tuorum

fata tibi; cernes urbem et promissa Lavini

moenia, sublimemque feres ad sidera caeli

260   magnanimum Aenean; neque me sententia vertit.

Hic tibi (fabor enim, quando haec te cura remordet,

longius et volvens fatorum arcana movebo)

bellum ingens geret Italia populosque feroces

contundet moresque viris et moenia ponet,

265   tertia dum Latio regnantem viderit aestas,

ternaque transierint Rutulis hiberna subactis.

At puer Ascanius, cui nunc cognomen Iulo

additur (Ilus erat, dum res stetit Ilia regno),

triginta magnos volvendis mensibus orbis

270   imperio explebit, regnumque ab sede Lavini

transferet, et Longam multa vi muniet Albam.

Hic iam ter centum totos regnabitur annos

gente sub Hectorea, donec regina sacerdos

Marte gravis geminam partu dabit Ilia prolem.

275   Inde lupae fulvo nutricis tegmine laetus

Romulus excipiet gentem et Mavortia condet

moenia Romanosque suo de nomine dicet.

His ego nec metas rerum nec tempora pono:

imperium sine fine dedi. Quin aspera Iuno,

280   quae mare nunc terrasque metu caelumque fatigat,

consilia in melius referet, mecumque fovebit

Romanos, rerum dominos gentemque togatam.

Sic placitum. Veniet lustris labentibus aetas

cum domus Assaraci Phthiam clarasque Mycenas

servitio premet ac victis dominabitur Argis.   285

Nascetur pulchra Troianus origine Caesar,

imperium Oceano, famam qui terminet astris,

Iulius, a magno demissum nomen Iulo.

Hunc tu olim caelo spoliis Orientis onustum

accipies secura; vocabitur hic quoque votis.   290

Aspera tum positis mitescent saecula bellis;

cana Fides et Vesta, Remo cum fratre Quirinus

iura dabunt; dirae ferro et compagibus artis

claudentur Belli portae; Furor impius intus

saeva sedens super arma et centum vinctus aenis   295

post tergum nodis fremet horridus ore cruento."

Haec ait et Maia genitum demittit ab alto,

ut terrae utque novae pateant Karthaginis arces

hospitio Teucris, ne fati nescia Dido

finibus arceret. Volat ille per aera magnum   300

remigio alarum ac Libyae citus astitit oris.

Et iam iussa facit, ponuntque ferocia Poeni

corda volente deo; in primis regina quietum

accipit in Teucros animum mentemque benignam.

At pius Aeneas per noctem plurima volvens,   305

ut primum lux alma data est, exire locosque

explorare novos, quas vento accesserit oras,

qui teneant (nam inculta videt), hominesne feraene,

quaerere constituit sociisque exacta referre.

310   Classem in convexo nemorum sub rupe cavata

arboribus clausam circum atque horrentibus umbris

occulit; ipse uno graditur comitatus Achate

bina manu lato crispans hastilia ferro.

Cui mater media sese tulit obvia silva

315   virginis os habitumque gerens et virginis arma

Spartanae, vel qualis equos Threissa fatigat

Harpalyce volucremque fuga praevertitur Hebrum.

Namque umeris de more habilem suspenderat arcum

venatrix dederatque comam diffundere ventis,

320   nuda genu nodoque sinus collecta fluentes.

Ac prior "Heus," inquit, "iuvenes, monstrate, mearum

vidistis si quam hic errantem forte sororum

succinctam pharetra et maculosae tegmine lyncis,

aut spumantis apri cursum clamore prementem."

325   Sic Venus et Veneris contra sic filius orsus:

"Nulla tuarum audita mihi neque visa sororum,

O quam te memorem, virgo? Namque haud tibi vultus

mortalis, nec vox hominem sonat; O, dea certe

(an Phoebi soror? An Nympharum sanguinis una?),

sis felix nostrumque leves, quaecumque, laborem 330

et quo sub caelo tandem, quibus orbis in oris

iactemur doceas: ignari hominumque locorumque

erramus vento huc vastis et fluctibus acti:

multa tibi ante aras nostra cadet hostia dextra."

Tum Venus: "Haud equidem tali me dignor honore; 335

virginibus Tyriis mos est gestare pharetram

purpureoque alte suras vincire coturno.

Punica regna vides, Tyrios et Agenoris urbem;

sed fines Libyci, genus intractabile bello.

Imperium Dido Tyria regit urbe profecta, 340

germanum fugiens. Longa est iniuria, longae

ambages; sed summa sequar fastigia rerum.

Huic coniunx Sychaeus erat, ditissimus auri

Phoenicum, et magno miserae dilectus amore,

cui pater intactam dederat primisque iugarat 345

ominibus. Sed regna Tyri germanus habebat

Pygmalion, scelere ante alios immanior omnes.

Quos inter medius venit furor. Ille Sychaeum

impius ante aras atque auri caecus amore

clam ferro incautum superat, securus amorum 350

germanae; factumque diu celavit et aegram

multa malus simulans vana spe lusit amantem.

Ipsa sed in somnis inhumati venit imago

coniugis ora modis attollens pallida miris;

355 crudeles aras traiectaque pectora ferro

nudavit, caecumque domus scelus omne retexit.

Tum celerare fugam patriaque excedere suadet

auxiliumque viae veteres tellure recludit

thesauros, ignotum argenti pondus et auri.

360 His commota fugam Dido sociosque parabat.

Conveniunt quibus aut odium crudele tyranni

aut metus acer erat; naves, quae forte paratae,

corripiunt onerantque auro. Portantur avari

Pygmalionis opes pelago; dux femina facti.

365 Devenere locos ubi nunc ingentia cernes

moenia surgentemque novae Karthaginis arcem,

mercatique solum, facti de nomine Byrsam,

taurino quantum possent circumdare tergo.

Sed vos qui tandem? Quibus aut venistis ab oris?

370 Quove tenetis iter?" Quaerenti talibus ille

suspirans imoque trahens a pectore vocem:

"O dea, si prima repetens ab origine pergam

et vacet annales nostrorum audire laborum,

ante diem clauso componet Vesper Olympo.

375 Nos Troia antiqua, si vestras forte per aures

Troiae nomen iit, diversa per aequora vectos

forte sua Libycis tempestas appulit oris.

Sum pius Aeneas, raptos qui ex hoste penates

classe veho mecum, fama super aethera notus;

Italiam quaero patriam, et genus ab Iove summo.   380

Bis denis Phrygium conscendi navibus aequor,

matre dea monstrante viam data fata secutus;

vix septem convulsae undis Euroque supersunt.

Ipse ignotus, egens, Libyae deserta peragro,

Europa atque Asia pulsus." Nec plura querentem   385

passa Venus medio sic interfata dolore est:

"Quisquis es, haud, credo, invisus caelestibus auras

vitales carpis, Tyriam qui adveneris urbem;

perge modo atque hinc te reginae ad limina perfer.

Namque tibi reduces socios classemque relatam   390

nuntio et in tutum versis Aquilonibus actam,

ni frustra augurium vani docuere parentes.

Aspice bis senos laetantes agmine cycnos,

aetheria quos lapsa plaga Iovis ales aperto

turbabat caelo; nunc terras ordine longo   395

aut capere aut captas iam despectare videntur:

ut reduces illi ludunt stridentibus alis

et coetu cinxere polum cantusque dedere,

haud aliter puppesque tuae pubesque tuorum

aut portum tenet aut pleno subit ostia velo.   400

Perge modo et, qua te ducit via, derige gressum."

Dixit et avertens rosea cervice refulsit,

ambrosiaeque comae divinum vertice odorem

spiravere; pedes vestis defluxit ad imos,

405   et vera incessu patuit dea. Ille ubi matrem

agnovit tali fugientem est voce secutus:

"Quid natum totiens, crudelis tu quoque, falsis

ludis imaginibus? Cur dextrae iungere dextram

non datur ac veras audire et reddere voces?"

410   Talibus incusat gressumque ad moenia tendit.

At Venus obscuro gradientes aere saepsit,

et multo nebulae circum dea fudit amictu,

cernere ne quis eos neu quis contingere posset

molirive moram aut veniendi poscere causas.

415   Ipsa Paphum sublimis abit sedesque revisit

laeta suas, ubi templum illi, centumque Sabaeo

ture calent arae sertisque recentibus halant.

Corripuere viam interea, qua semita monstrat.

Iamque ascendebant collem, qui plurimus urbi

420   imminet adversasque aspectat desuper arces.

Miratur molem Aeneas, magalia quondam,

miratur portas strepitumque et strata viarum.

Instant ardentes Tyrii: pars ducere muros

molirique arcem et manibus subvolvere saxa,

425   pars optare locum tecto et concludere sulco;

iura magistratusque legunt sanctumque senatum.

Hic portus alii effodiunt; hic alta theatris

fundamenta locant alii, immanesque columnas

rupibus excidunt, scaenis decora alta futuris.

Qualis apes aestate nova per florea rura   430

exercet sub sole labor, cum gentis adultos

educunt fetus, aut cum liquentia mella

stipant et dulci distendunt nectare cellas,

aut onera accipiunt venientum, aut agmine facto

ignavum fucos pecus a praesepibus arcent;   435

fervet opus redolentque thymo fraglantia mella.

"O fortunati, quorum iam moenia surgunt!"

Aeneas ait et fastigia suspicit urbis.

Infert se saeptus nebula (mirabile dictu)

per medios, miscetque viris neque cernitur ulli.   440

Lucus in urbe fuit media, laetissimus umbrae,

quo primum iactati undis et turbine Poeni

effodere loco signum, quod regia Iuno

monstrarat, caput acris equi; sic nam fore bello

egregiam et facilem victu per saecula gentem.   445

Hic templum Iunoni ingens Sidonia Dido

condebat, donis opulentum et numine divae,

aerea cui gradibus surgebant limina nexaeque

aere trabes, foribus cardo stridebat aenis.

450 Hoc primum in luco nova res oblata timorem

leniit, hic primum Aeneas sperare salutem

ausus et adflictis melius confidere rebus.

Namque sub ingenti lustrat dum singula templo

reginam opperiens, dum quae fortuna sit urbi

455 artificumque manus inter se operumque laborem

miratur, videt Iliacas ex ordine pugnas

bellaque iam fama totum vulgata per orbem,

Atridas Priamumque et saevum ambobus Achillem.

Constitit et lacrimans "Quis iam locus," inquit, "Achate,

460 quae regio in terris nostri non plena laboris?

En Priamus. Sunt hic etiam sua praemia laudi,

sunt lacrimae rerum et mentem mortalia tangunt.

Solve metus; feret haec aliquam tibi fama salutem."

Sic ait atque animum pictura pascit inani

465 multa gemens, largoque umectat flumine vultum.

Namque videbat uti bellantes Pergama circum

hac fugerent Grai, premeret Troiana iuventus;

hac Phryges, instaret curru cristatus Achilles.

Nec procul hinc Rhesi niveis tentoria velis

470 agnoscit lacrimans, primo quae prodita somno

Ty–dides multa vastabat caede cruentus,

ardentesque avertit equos in castra prius quam

pabula gustassent Troiae Xanthumque bibissent.

Parte alia fugiens amissis Troilus armis,

infelix puer atque impar congressus Achilli,   475

fertur equis curruque haeret resupinus inani,

lora tenens tamen; huic cervixque comaeque trahuntur

per terram, et versa pulvis inscribitur hasta.

Interea ad templum non aequae Palladis ibant

crinibus Iliades passis peplumque ferebant   480

suppliciter, tristes et tunsae pectora palmis;

diva solo fixos oculos aversa tenebat.

Ter circum Iliacos raptaverat Hectora muros

exanimumque auro corpus vendebat Achilles.

Tum vero ingentem gemitum dat pectore ab imo,   485

ut spolia, ut currus, utque ipsum corpus amici

tendentemque manus Priamum conspexit inermes.

Se quoque principibus permixtum agnovit Achivis,

Eoasque acies et nigri Memnonis arma.

Ducit Amazonidum lunatis agmina peltis   490

Penthesilea furens mediisque in milibus ardet,

aurea subnectens exsertae cingula mammae

bellatrix, audetque viris concurrere virgo.

Haec dum Dardanio Aeneae miranda videntur,

dum stupet obtutuque haeret defixus in uno,   495

regina ad templum, forma pulcherrima Dido,

incessit magna iuvenum stipante caterva.

Qualis in Eurotae ripis aut per iuga Cynthi

exercet Diana choros, quam mille secutae

500 hinc atque hinc glomerantur Oreades; illa pharetram

fert umero gradiensque deas supereminet omnes

(Latonae tacitum pertemptant gaudia pectus):

talis erat Dido, talem se laeta ferebat

per medios instans operi regnisque futuris.

505 Tum foribus divae, media testudine templi,

saepta armis solioque alte subnixa resedit.

Iura dabat legesque viris, operumque laborem

partibus aequabat iustis aut sorte trahebat:

cum subito Aeneas concursu accedere magno

510 Anthea Sergestumque videt fortemque Cloanthum

Teucrorumque alios, ater quos aequore turbo

dispulerat penitusque alias avexerat oras.

Obstipuit simul ipse, simul percussus Achates

laetitiaque metuque; avidi coniungere dextras

515 ardebant, sed res animos incognita turbat.

Dissimulant et nube cava speculantur amicti

quae fortuna viris, classem quo litore linquant,

quid veniant; cunctis nam lecti navibus ibant

orantes veniam et templum clamore petebant.

CONTICUERE omnes intentique ora tenebant;

inde toro pater Aeneas sic orsus ab alto:

"Infandum, regina, iubes renovare dolorem,

Troianas ut opes et lamentabile regnum

eruerint Danai, quaeque ipse miserrima vidi   5

et quorum pars magna fui. Quis talia fando

Myrmidonum Dolopumve aut duri miles Ulixi

temperet a lacrimis? Et iam nox umida caelo

praecipitat suadentque cadentia sidera somnos.

Sed si tantus amor casus cognoscere nostros   10

et breviter Troiae supremum audire laborem,

quamquam animus meminisse horret luctuque refugit

incipiam. Fracti bello fatisque repulsi

ductores Danaum tot iam labentibus annis

instar montis equum divina Palladis arte   15

aedificant, sectaque intexunt abiete costas;

votum pro reditu simulant; ea fama vagatur.

Huc delecta virum sortiti corpora furtim

includunt caeco lateri penitusque cavernas

ingentes uterumque armato milite complent.   20

Est in conspectu Tenedos, notissima fama

insula, dives opum Priami dum regna manebant,

nunc tantum sinus et statio male fida carinis:

huc se provecti deserto in litore condunt;

25 nos abiisse rati et vento petiisse Mycenas.

Ergo omnis longo solvit se Teucria luctu;

panduntur portae, iuvat ire et Dorica castra

desertosque videre locos litusque relictum:

hic Dolopum manus, hic saevus tendebat Achilles;

30 classibus hic locus, hic acie certare solebant.

Pars stupet innuptae donum exitiale Minervae

et molem mirantur equi; primusque Thymoetes

duci intra muros hortatur et arce locari,

sive dolo seu iam Troiae sic fata ferebant.

35 At Capys, et quorum melior sententia menti,

aut pelago Danaum insidias suspectaque dona

praecipitare iubent subiectisque urere flammis,

aut terebrare cavas uteri et temptare latebras.

Scinditur incertum studia in contraria vulgus.

40 Primus ibi ante omnes magna comitante caterva

Laocoon ardens summa decurrit ab arce,

et procul 'O miseri, quae tanta insania, cives?

Creditis avectos hostes? Aut ulla putatis

dona carere dolis Danaum? Sic notus Ulixes?

45 Aut hoc inclusi ligno occultantur Achivi,

aut haec in nostros fabricata est machina muros,

inspectura domos venturaque desuper urbi,

aut aliquis latet error; equo ne credite, Teucri.

Quidquid id est, timeo Danaos et dona ferentes.'

Sic fatus validis ingentem viribus hastam   50

in latus inque feri curvam compagibus alvum

contorsit. Stetit illa tremens, uteroque recusso

insonuere cavae gemitumque dedere cavernae.

Et, si fata deum, si mens non laeva fuisset,

impulerat ferro Argolicas foedare latebras,   55

Troiaque nunc staret, Priamique arx alta maneres.

BOOK 2.199–297

Hic aliud maius miseris multoque tremendum

200 obicitur magis atque improvida pectora turbat.

Laocoon, ductus Neptuno sorte sacerdos,

sollemnes taurum ingentem mactabat ad aras.

Ecce autem gemini a Tenedo tranquilla per alta

(horresco referens) immensis orbibus angues

205 incumbunt pelago pariterque ad litora tendunt;

pectora quorum inter fluctus arrecta iubaeque

sanguineae superant undas, pars cetera pontum

pone legit sinuatque immensa volumine terga.

Fit sonitus spumante salo; iamque arva tenebant

210 ardentesque oculos suffecti sanguine et igni

sibila lambebant linguis vibrantibus ora.

Diffugimus visu exsangues. Illi agmine certo

Laocoonta petunt; et primum parva duorum

corpora natorum serpens amplexus uterque

215 implicat et miseros morsu depascitur artus;

post ipsum auxilio subeuntem ac tela ferentem

corripiunt spirisque ligant ingentibus; et iam

bis medium amplexi, bis collo squamea circum

terga dati superant capite et cervicibus altis.

220 Ille simul manibus tendit divellere nodos

perfusus sanie vittas atroque veneno,

clamores simul horrendos ad sidera tollit:

qualis mugitus, fugit cum saucius aram

taurus et incertam excussit cervice securim.

At gemini lapsu delubra ad summa dracones   225

effugiunt saevaeque petunt Tritonidis arcem,

sub pedibusque deae clipeique sub orbe teguntur.

Tum vero tremefacta novus per pectora cunctis

insinuat pavor, et scelus expendisse merentem

Laocoonta ferunt, sacrum qui cuspide robur   230

laeserit et tergo sceleratam intorserit hastam.

Ducendum ad sedes simulacrum orandaque divae

numina conclamant.

Dividimus muros et moenia pandimus urbis.

Accingunt omnes operi pedibusque rotarum   235

subiciunt lapsus, et stuppea vincula collo

intendunt: scandit fatalis machina muros

feta armis. Pueri circum innuptaeque puellae

sacra canunt funemque manu contingere gaudent;

illa subit mediaeque minans inlabitur urbi.   240

O patria, O divum domus Ilium et incluta bello

moenia Dardanidum! quater ipso in limine portae

substitit atque utero sonitum quater arma dedere;

instamus tamen immemores caecique furore

245   et monstrum infelix sacrata sistimus arce.

      Tunc etiam fatis aperit Cassandra futuris

      ora dei iussu non umquam credita Teucris.

      Nos delubra deum miseri, quibus ultimus esset

      ille dies, festa velamus fronde per urbem.

250   Vertitur interea caelum et ruit Oceano nox

      involvens umbra magna terramque polumque

      Myrmidonumque dolos; fusi per moenia Teucri

      conticuere; sopor fessos complectitur artus.

      Et iam Argiva phalanx instructis navibus ibat

255   a Tenedo tacitae per amica silentia lunae

      litora nota petens, flammas cum regia puppis

      extulerat, fatisque deum defensus iniquis

      inclusos utero Danaos et pinea furtim

      laxat claustra Sinon. Illos patefactus ad auras

260   reddit equus laetique cavo se robore promunt

      Thessandrus Sthenelusque duces et dirus Ulixes,

      demissum lapsi per funem, Acamasque Thoasque

      Pelidesque Neoptolemus primusque Machaon

      et Menelaus et ipse doli fabricator Epeos.

265   Invadunt urbem somno vinoque sepultam;

      caeduntur vigiles, portisque patentibus omnes

      accipiunt socios atque agmina conscia iungunt.

      Tempus erat quo prima quies mortalibus aegris

incipit et dono divum gratissima serpit.

In somnis, ecce, ante oculos maestissimus Hector   270

visus adesse mihi largosque effundere fletus,

raptatus bigis ut quondam, aterque cruento

pulvere perque pedes traiectus lora tumentes.

Ei mihi, qualis erat, quantum mutatus ab illo

Hectore qui redit exuvias indutus Achilli   275

vel Danaum Phrygios iaculatus puppibus ignes;

squalentem barbam et concretos sanguine crines

vulneraque illa gerens, quae circum plurima muros

accepit patrios. Ultro flens ipse videbar

compellare virum et maestas expromere voces: 280

'O lux Dardaniae, spes O fidissima Teucrum,

quae tantae tenuere morae? Quibus Hector ab oris

exspectate venis? Ut te post multa tuorum

funera, post varios hominumque urbisque labores

defessi aspicimus! Quae causa indigna serenos   285

foedavit vultus? Aut cur haec vulnera cerno?'

Ille nihil, nec me quaerentem vana moratur,

sed graviter gemitus imo de pectore ducens,

'Heu fuge, nate dea, teque his' ait 'eripe flammis.

Hostis habet muros; ruit alto a culmine Troia.   290

Sat patriae Priamoque datum: si Pergama dextra

defendi possent, etiam hac defensa fuissent.

Sacra suosque tibi commendat Troia penates;

hos cape fatorum comites, his moenia quaere

295 magna, pererrato statues quae denique ponto.'

Sic ait et manibus vittas Vestamque potentem

aeternumque adytis effert penetralibus ignem.

Vestibulum ante ipsum primoque in limine Pyrrhus

exsultat telis et luce coruscus aena: 470

qualis ubi in lucem coluber mala gramina pastus,

frigida sub terra tumidum quem bruma tegebat,

nunc, positis novus exuviis nitidusque iuventa,

lubrica convolvit sublato pectore terga

arduus ad solem, et linguis micat ore trisulcis. 475

Una ingens Periphas et equorum agitator Achillis,

armiger Automedon, una omnis Scyria pubes

succedunt tecto et flammas ad culmina iactant.

Ipse inter primos correpta dura bipenni

limina perrumpit postesque a cardine vellit 480

aeratos; iamque excisa trabe firma cavavit

robora et ingentem lato dedit ore fenestram.

Apparet domus intus et atria longa patescunt;

apparent Priami et veterum penetralia regum,

armatosque vident stantes in limine primo. 485

At domus interior gemitu miseroque tumultu

miscetur, penitusque cavae plangoribus aedes

femineis ululant; ferit aurea sidera clamor.

Tum pavidae tectis matres ingentibus errant

amplexaeque tenent postes atque oscula figunt. 490

Instat vi patria Pyrrhus; nec claustra nec ipsi

custodes sufferre valent; labat ariete crebro

ianua, et emoti procumbunt cardine postes.

Fit via vi; rumpunt aditus primosque trucidant

495   immissi Danai et late loca milite complent.

Non sic, aggeribus ruptis cum spumeus amnis

exiit oppositasque evicit gurgite moles,

fertur in arva furens cumulo camposque per omnes

cum stabulis armenta trahit. Vidi ipse furentem

500   caede Neoptolemum geminosque in limine Atridas,

vidi Hecubam centumque nurus Priamumque per aras

sanguine foedantem quos ipse sacraverat ignes.

Quinquaginta illi thalami, spes tanta nepotum,

barbarico postes auro spoliisque superbi

505   procubuere; tenent Danai qua deficit ignis.

Forsitan et Priami fuerint quae fata requiras.

Urbis uti captae casum convulsaque vidit

limina tectorum et medium in penetralibus hostem,

arma diu senior desueta trementibus aevo

510   circumdat nequiquam umeris et inutile ferrum

cingitur, ac densos fertur moriturus in hostes.

Aedibus in mediis nudoque sub aetheris axe

ingens ara fuit iuxtaque veterrima laurus

incumbens arae atque umbra complexa penates.

Hic Hecuba et natae nequiquam altaria circum,   515

praecipites atra ceu tempestate columbae,

condensae et divum amplexae simulacra sedebant.

Ipsum autem sumptis Priamum iuvenalibus armis

ut vidit, 'Quae mens tam dira, miserrime coniunx,

impulit his cingi telis? Aut quo ruis?' inquit.   520

'Non tali auxilio nec defensoribus istis

tempus eget; non, si ipse meus nunc adforet Hector.

Huc tandem concede; haec ara tuebitur omnes,

aut moriere simul.' Sic ore effata recepit

ad sese et sacra longaevum in sede locavit.   525

Ecce autem elapsus Pyrrhi de caede Polites,

unus natorum Priami, per tela, per hostes

porticibus longis fugit et vacua atria lustrat

saucius. Illum ardens infesto vulnere Pyrrhus

insequitur, iam iamque manu tenet et premit hasta.   530

Ut tandem ante oculos evasit et ora parentum,

concidit ac multo vitam cum sanguine fudit.

Hic Priamus, quamquam in media iam morte tenetur,

non tamen abstinuit nec voci iraeque pepercit:

'At tibi pro scelere,' exclamat, 'pro talibus ausis   535

di, si qua est caelo pietas quae talia curet,

persolvant grates dignas et praemia reddant

debita, qui nati coram me cernere letum

fecisti et patrios foedasti funere vultus.

540   At non ille, satum quo te mentiris, Achilles

talis in hoste fuit Priamo; sed iura fidemque

supplicis erubuit corpusque exsangue sepulcro

reddidit Hectoreum meque in mea regna remisit.'

Sic fatus senior telumque imbelle sine ictu

545   coniecit, rauco quod protinus aere repulsum,

et summo clipei nequiquam umbone pependit.

Cui Pyrrhus: 'Referes ergo haec et nuntius ibis

Pelidae genitori. Illi mea tristia facta

degeneremque Neoptolemum narrare memento.

550   Nunc morere.' Hoc dicens altaria ad ipsa trementem

traxit et in multo lapsantem sanguine nati,

implicuitque comam laeva, dextraque coruscum

extulit ac lateri capulo tenus abdidit ensem.

Haec finis Priami fatorum, hic exitus illum

555   sorte tulit Troiam incensam et prolapsa videntem

Pergama, tot quondam populis terrisque superbum

regnatorem Asiae. Iacet ingens litore truncus,

avulsumque umeris caput et sine nomine corpus.

At me tum primum saevus circumstetit horror.

560   Obstipui; subiit cari genitoris imago,

ut regem aequaevum crudeli vulnere vidi

vitam exhalantem, subiit deserta Creusa

et direpta domus et parvi casus Iuli.

Respicio et quae sit me circum copia lustro.

Deseruere omnes defessi, et corpora saltu 565

ad terram misere aut ignibus aegra dedere.

735   Hic mihi nescio quod trepido male numen amicum

confusam eripuit mentem. Namque avia cursu

dum sequor et nota excedo regione viarum,

heu misero coniunx fatone erepta Creusa

substitit, erravitne via seu lapsa resedit,

740   incertum; nec post oculis est reddita nostris.

Nec prius amissam respexi animumve reflexi

quam tumulum antiquae Cereris sedemque sacratam

venimus: hic demum collectis omnibus una

defuit, et comites natumque virumque fefellit.

745   Quem non incusavi amens hominumque deorumque,

aut quid in eversa vidi crudelius urbe?

Ascanium Anchisenque patrem Teucrosque penates

commendo sociis et curva valle recondo;

ipse urbem repeto et cingor fulgentibus armis.

750   Stat casus renovare omnes omnemque reverti

per Troiam et rursus caput obiectare periclis.

Principio muros obscuraque limina portae,

qua gressum extuleram, repeto et vestigia retro

observata sequor per noctem et lumine lustro:

755   horror ubique animo, simul ipsa silentia terrent.

Inde domum, si forte pedem, si forte tulisset,

me refero: inruerant Danai et tectum omne tenebant.

Ilicet ignis edax summa ad fastigia vento

volvitur; exsuperant flammae, furit aestus ad auras.

Procedo et Priami sedes arcemque reviso: 760

et iam porticibus vacuis Iunonis asylo

custodes lecti Phoenix et dirus Ulixes

praedam adservabant. Huc undique Troia gaza

incensis erepta adytis, mensaeque deorum

crateresque auro solidi, captivaque vestis   765

congeritur. Pueri et pavidae longo ordine matres

stant circum.

Ausus quin etiam voces iactare per umbram

implevi clamore vias, maestusque Creusam

nequiquam ingeminans iterumque iterumque vocavi.   770

Quaerenti et tectis urbis sine fine ruenti

infelix simulacrum atque ipsius umbra Creusae

visa mihi ante oculos et nota maior imago.

Obstipui, steteruntque comae et vox faucibus haesit.

Tum sic adfari et curas his demere dictis: 775

'Quid tantum insano iuvat indulgere dolori,

O dulcis coniunx? Non haec sine numine divum

eveniunt; nec te comitem hinc portare Creusam

fas, aut ille sinit superi regnator Olympi.

Longa tibi exsilia et vastum maris aequor arandum,   780 et terram Hesperiam venies, ubi Lydius arva

inter opima virum leni fluit agmine Thybris.

illic res laetae regnumque et regia coniunx

parta tibi; lacrimas dilectae pelle Creusae.

785 Non ego Myrmidonum sedes Dolopumve superbas

aspiciam aut Grais servitum matribus ibo,

Dardanis et divae Veneris nurus;

sed me magna deum genetrix his detinet oris.

Iamque vale et nati serva communis amorem.'

790 Haec ubi dicta dedit, lacrimantem et multa volentem

dicere deseruit, tenuesque recessit in auras.

Ter conatus ibi collo dare bracchia circum;

ter frustra comprensa manus effugit imago,

par levibus ventis volucrique simillima somno.

795 Sic demum socios consumpta nocte reviso.

Atque hic ingentem comitum adfluxisse novorum

invenio admirans numerum, matresque virosque,

collectam exsilio pubem, miserabile vulgus.

Undique convenere animis opibusque parati

800 in quascumque velim pelago deducere terras.

Iamque iugis summae surgebat Lucifer Idae

ducebatque diem, Danaique obsessa tenebant

limina portarum, nec spes opis ulla dabatur.

Cessi et sublato montes genitore petivi.

At regina gravi iamdudum saucia cura

vulnus alit venis et caeco carpitur igni.

Multa viri virtus animo multusque recursat

gentis honos; haerent infixi pectore vultus

verbaque nec placidam membris dat cura quietem.   5

Postera Phoebea lustrabat lampade terras

umentemque Aurora polo dimoverat umbram,

cum sic unanimam adloquitur male sana sororem:

"Anna soror, quae me suspensam insomnia terrent!

Quis novus hic nostris successit sedibus hospes,   10

quem sese ore ferens, quam forti pectore et armis!

Credo equidem, nec vana fides, genus esse deorum.

Degeneres animos timor arguit. Heu, quibus ille

iactatus fatis! Quae bella exhausta canebat!

Si mihi non animo fixum immotumque sederet   15

ne cui me vinclo vellem sociare iugali,

postquam primus amor deceptam morte fefellit;

si non pertaesum thalami taedaeque fuisset,

huic uni forsan potui succumbere culpae.

Anna (fatebor enim) miseri post fata Sychaei   20

coniugis et sparsos fraterna caede penates

solus hic inflexit sensus animumque labantem

impulit. Agnosco veteris vestigia flammae.

Sed mihi vel tellus optem prius ima dehiscat

25   vel pater omnipotens adigat me fulmine ad umbras,

pallentes umbras Erebo noctemque profundam,

ante, pudor, quam te violo aut tua iura resolvo.

Ille meos, primus qui me sibi iunxit, amores

abstulit; ille habeat secum servetque sepulcro."

30   Sic effata sinum lacrimis implevit obortis.

Anna refert: "O luce magis dilecta sorori,

solane perpetua maerens carpere iuventa

nec dulces natos Veneris nec praemia noris?

Id cinerem aut manes credis curare sepultos?

35   Esto: aegram nulli quondam flexere mariti,

non Libyae, non ante Tyro; despectus Iarbas

ductoresque alii, quos Africa terra triumphis

dives alit: placitone etiam pugnabis amori?

Nec venit in mentem quorum consederis arvis?

40   Hinc Gaetulae urbes, genus insuperabile bello,

et Numidae infreni cingunt et inhospita Syrtis;

hinc deserta siti regio lateque furentes

Barcaei. Quid bella Tyro surgentia dicam

germanique minas?

45   Dis equidem auspicibus reor et Iunone secunda

hunc cursum Iliacas vento tenuisse carinas.

Quam tu urbem, soror, hanc cernes, quae surgere regna

coniugio tali! Teucrum comitantibus armis

Punica se quantis attollet gloria rebus!

Tu modo posce deos veniam, sacrisque litatis   50

indulge hospitio causasque innecte morandi,

dum pelago desaevit hiems et aquosus Orion,

quassataeque rates, dum non tractabile caelum."

His dictis impenso animum flammavit amore

spemque dedit dubiae menti solvitque pudorem.   55

Principio delubra adeunt pacemque per aras

exquirunt; mactant lectas de more bidentes

legiferae Cereri Phoeboque patrique Lyaeo,

Iunoni ante omnes, cui vincla iugalia curae.

Ipsa tenens dextra pateram pulcherrima Dido   60

candentis vaccae media inter cornua fundit,

aut ante ora deum pingues spatiatur ad aras,

instauratque diem donis, pecudumque reclusis

pectoribus inhians spirantia consulit exta.

Heu, vatum ignarae mentes! Quid vota furentem,   65

quid delubra iuvant? Est molles flamma medullas

interea et tacitum vivit sub pectore vulnus.

Uritur infelix Dido totaque vagatur

urbe furens, qualis coniecta cerva sagitta,

quam procul incautam nemora inter Cresia fixit   70 pastor agens telis liquitque volatile ferrum

nescius: illa fuga silvas saltusque peragrat

Dictaeos; haeret lateri letalis harundo.

Nunc media Aenean secum per moenia ducit

75   Sidoniasque ostentat opes urbemque paratam,

incipit effari mediaque in voce resistit;

nunc eadem labente die convivia quaerit,

Iliacosque iterum demens audire labores

exposcit pendetque iterum narrantis ab ore.

80   Post ubi digressi, lumenque obscura vicissim

luna premit suadentque cadentia sidera somnos,

sola domo maeret vacua stratisque relictis

incubat. Illum absens absentem auditque videtque,

aut gremio Ascanium genitoris imagine capta

85   detinet, infandum si fallere possit amorem.

Non coeptae adsurgunt turres, non arma iuventus

exercet portusve aut propugnacula bello

tuta parant: pendent opera interrupta minaeque

murorum ingentes aequataque machina caelo.

90   Quam simul ac tali persensit peste teneri

cara Iovis coniunx nec famam obstare furori,

talibus adgreditur Venerem Saturnia dictis:

"Egregiam vero laudem et spolia ampla refertis

tuque puerque tuus (magnum et memorabile numen),

una dolo divum si femina victa duorum est.   95

Nec me adeo fallit veritam te moenia nostra

suspectas habuisse domos Karthaginis altae.

Sed quis erit modus, aut quo nunc certamine tanto?

Quin potius pacem aeternam pactosque hymenaeos

exercemus? Habes tota quod mente petisti: 100

ardet amans Dido traxitque per ossa furorem.

Communem hunc ergo populum paribusque regamus

auspiciis; liceat Phrygio servire marito

dotalesque tuae Tyrios permittere dextrae."

Olli (sensit enim simulata mente locutam,   105

quo regnum Italiae Libycas averteret oras)

sic contra est ingressa Venus: "Quis talia demens

abnuat aut tecum malit contendere bello?

Si modo quod memoras factum fortuna sequatur.

Sed fatis incerta feror, si Iuppiter unam   110

esse velit Tyriis urbem Troiaque profectis,

miscerive probet populos aut foedera iungi.

Tu coniunx, tibi fas animum temptare precando.

Perge, sequar." Tum sic excepit regia Iuno:

"Mecum erit iste labor. Nunc qua ratione quod instat   115

confieri possit, paucis (adverte) docebo.

Venatum Aeneas unaque miserrima Dido

in nemus ire parant, ubi primos crastinus ortus

extulerit Titan radiisque retexerit orbem.

120 His ego nigrantem commixta grandine nimbum,

dum trepidant alae saltusque indagine cingunt,

desuper infundam et tonitru caelum omne ciebo.

Diffugient comites et nocte tegentur opaca:

speluncam Dido dux et Troianus eandem

125 devenient. Adero et, tua si mihi certa voluntas,

conubio iungam stabili propriamque dicabo.

Hic hymenaeus erit." Non adversata petenti

adnuit atque dolis risit Cytherea repertis.

Oceanum interea surgens Aurora reliquit.

130 It portis iubare exorto delecta iuventus,

retia rara, plagae, lato venabula ferro,

Massylique ruunt equites et odora canum vis.

Reginam thalamo cunctantem ad limina primi

Poenorum exspectant, ostroque insignis et auro

135 stat sonipes ac frena ferox spumantia mandit.

Tandem progreditur magna stipante caterva

Sidoniam picto chlamydem circumdata limbo;

cui pharetra ex auro, crines nodantur in aurum,

aurea purpuream subnectit fibula vestem.

140 Nec non et Phrygii comites et laetus Iulus

incedunt. Ipse ante alios pulcherrimus omnes

infert se socium Aeneas atque agmina iungit.

Qualis ubi hibernam Lyciam Xanthique fluenta

deserit ac Delum maternam invisit Apollo

instauratque choros, mixtique altaria circum 145

Cretesque Dryopesque fremunt pictique Agathyrsi;

ipse iugis Cynthi graditur mollique fluentem

fronde premit crinem fingens atque implicat auro,

tela sonant umeris: haud illo segnior ibat

Aeneas, tantum egregio decus enitet ore. 150

Postquam altos ventum in montes atque invia lustra,

ecce ferae saxi deiectae vertice caprae

decurrere iugis; alia de parte patentes

transmittunt cursu campos atque agmina cervi

pulverulenta fuga glomerant montesque relinquunt. 155

At puer Ascanius mediis in vallibus acri

gaudet equo iamque hos cursu, iam praeterit illos,

spumantemque dari pecora inter inertia votis

optat aprum, aut fulvum descendere monte leonem.

Interea magno misceri murmure caelum 160

incipit, insequitur commixta grandine nimbus,

et Tyrii comites passim et Troiana iuventus

Dardaniusque nepos Veneris diversa per agros

tecta metu petiere; ruunt de montibus amnes.

Speluncam Dido dux et Troianus eandem 165

deveniunt. Prima et Tellus et pronuba Iuno

dant signum; fulsere ignes et conscius aether

conubiis summoque ulularunt vertice Nymphae.

Ille dies primus leti primusque malorum

170 causa fuit; neque enim specie famave movetur

nec iam furtivum Dido meditatur amorem:

coniugium vocat, hoc praetexit nomine culpam.

Extemplo Libyae magnas it Fama per urbes,

Fama, malum qua non aliud velocius ullum:

175 mobilitate viget viresque adquirit eundo,

parva metu primo, mox sese attollit in auras

ingrediturque solo et caput inter nubila condit.

Illam Terra parens ira inritata deorum

extremam, ut perhibent, Coeo Enceladoque sororem

180 progenuit pedibus celerem et pernicibus alis,

monstrum horrendum, ingens, cui quot sunt corpore plumae,

tot vigiles oculi subter (mirabile dictu),

tot linguae, totidem ora sonant, tot subrigit aures.

Nocte volat caeli medio terraeque per umbram

185 stridens, nec dulci declinat lumina somno;

luce sedet custos aut summi culmine tecti

turribus aut altis, et magnas territat urbes,

tam ficti pravique tenax quam nuntia veri.

Haec tum multiplici populos sermone replebat

190 gaudens, et pariter facta atque infecta canebat:

venisse Aenean Troiano sanguine cretum,

cui se pulchra viro dignetur iungere Dido;

nunc hiemem inter se luxu, quam longa, fovere

regnorum immemores turpique cupidine captos.

Haec passim dea foeda virum diffundit in ora.   195

Protinus ad regem cursus detorquet Iarban

incenditque animum dictis atque aggerat iras.

Hic Hammone satus rapta Garamantide nympha

templa Iovi centum latis immania regnis,

centum aras posuit vigilemque sacraverat ignem,   200

excubias divum aeternas, pecudumque cruore

pingue solum et variis florentia limina sertis.

Isque amens animi et rumore accensus amaro

dicitur ante aras media inter numina divum

multa Iovem manibus supplex orasse supinis: 205

"Iuppiter omnipotens, cui nunc Maurusia pictis

gens epulata toris Lenaeum libat honorem,

aspicis haec? An te, genitor, cum fulmina torques

nequiquam horremus, caecique in nubibus ignes

terrificant animos et inania murmura miscent?   210

Femina, quae nostris errans in finibus urbem

exiguam pretio posuit, cui litus arandum

cuique loci leges dedimus, conubia nostra

reppulit ac dominum Aenean in regna recepit.

215   Et nunc ille Paris cum semiviro comitatu,

Maeonia mentum mitra crinemque madentem

subnexus, rapto potitur: nos munera templis

quippe tuis ferimus famamque fovemus inanem."

Talibus orantem dictis arasque tenentem

220   audiit Omnipotens, oculosque ad moenia torsit

regia et oblitos famae melioris amantes.

Tum sic Mercurium adloquitur ac talia mandat:

"Vade age, nate, voca Zephyros et labere pennis

Dardaniumque ducem, Tyria Karthagine qui nunc

225   exspectat fatisque datas non respicit urbes,

adloquere et celeres defer mea dicta per auras.

Non illum nobis genetrix pulcherrima talem

promisit Graiumque ideo bis vindicat armis;

sed fore qui gravidam imperiis belloque frementem

230   Italiam regeret, genus alto a sanguine Teucri

proderet, ac totum sub leges mitteret orbem.

Si nulla accendit tantarum gloria rerum

nec super ipse sua molitur laude laborem,

Ascanione pater Romanas invidet arces?

235   Quid struit? Aut qua spe inimica in gente moratur

nec prolem Ausoniam et Lavinia respicit arva?

Naviget! Haec summa est, hic nostri nuntius esto."

Dixerat. Ille patris magni parere parabat

imperio; et primum pedibus talaria nectit

aurea, quae sublimem alis sive aequora supra 240

seu terram rapido pariter cum flamine portant.

Tum virgam capit: hac animas ille evocat Orco

pallentes, alias sub Tartara tristia mittit,

dat somnos adimitque, et lumina morte resignat.

Illa fretus agit ventos et turbida tranat 245

nubila. Iamque volans apicem et latera ardua cernit

Atlantis duri caelum qui vertice fulcit,

Atlantis, cinctum adsidue cui nubibus atris

piniferum caput et vento pulsatur et imbri,

nix umeros infusa tegit, tum flumina mento 250

praecipitant senis, et glacie riget horrida barba.

Hic primum paribus nitens Cyllenius alis

constitit; hinc toto praeceps se corpore ad undas

misit avi similis, quae circum litora, circum

piscosos scopulos humilis volat aequora iuxta. 255

Haud aliter terras inter caelumque volabat

litus harenosum ad Libyae, ventosque secabat

materno veniens ab avo Cyllenia proles.

Ut primum alatis tetigit magalia plantis,

Aenean fundantem arces ac tecta novantem 260

conspicit. Atque illi stellatus iaspide fulva

ensis erat Tyrioque ardebat murice laena

demissa ex umeris, dives quae munera Dido

fecerat, et tenui telas discreverat auro.

265   Continuo invadit: "Tu nunc Karthaginis altae

fundamenta locas pulchramque uxorius urbem

exstruis? Heu, regni rerumque oblite tuarum!

Ipse deum tibi me claro demittit Olympo

regnator, caelum et terras qui numine torquet,

270   ipse haec ferre iubet celeres mandata per auras:

Quid struis? Aut qua spe Libycis teris otia terris?

Si te nulla movet tantarum gloria rerum

[nec super ipse tua moliris laude laborem,]

Ascanium surgentem et spes heredis Iuli

275   respice, cui regnum Italiae Romanaque tellus

debetur." Tali Cyllenius ore locutus

mortales visus medio sermone reliquit

et procul in tenuem ex oculis evanuit auram.

At vero Aeneas aspectu obmutuit amens,

280   arrectaeque horrore comae et vox faucibus haesit.

Ardet abire fuga dulcesque relinquere terras,

attonitus tanto monitu imperioque deorum.

Heu quid agat? Quo nunc reginam ambire furentem

audeat adfatu? Quae prima exordia sumat?

285   Atque animum nunc huc celerem nunc dividit illuc

in partesque rapit varias perque omnia versat.

Haec alternanti potior sententia visa est:

Mnesthea Sergestumque vocat fortemque Serestum,

classem aptent taciti sociosque ad litora cogant,

arma parent et quae rebus sit causa novandis   290

dissimulent; sese interea, quando optima Dido

nesciat et tantos rumpi non speret amores,

temptaturum aditus et quae mollissima fandi

tempora, quis rebus dexter modus. Ocius omnes

imperio laeti parent et iussa facessunt.   295

At regina dolos (quis fallere possit amantem?)

praesensit, motusque excepit prima futuros

omnia tuta timens. Eadem impia Fama furenti

detulit armari classem cursumque parari.

Saevit inops animi totamque incensa per urbem   300

bacchatur, qualis commotis excita sacris

Thyias, ubi audito stimulant trieterica Baccho

orgia nocturnusque vocat clamore Cithaeron.

Tandem his Aenean compellat vocibus ultro:

"Dissimulare etiam sperasti, perfide, tantum   305

posse nefas tacitusque mea decedere terra?

Nec te noster amor nec te data dextera quondam

nec moritura tenet crudeli funere Dido?

Quin etiam hiberno moliri sidere classem

et mediis properas Aquilonibus ire per altum,   310 crudelis? Quid, si non arva aliena domosque

ignotas peteres, et Troia antiqua maneret,

Troia per undosum peteretur classibus aequor?

Mene fugis? Per ego has lacrimas dextramque tuam te

315   (quando aliud mihi iam miserae nihil ipsa reliqui),

per conubia nostra, per inceptos hymenaeos,

si bene quid de te merui, fuit aut tibi quicquam

dulce meum, miserere domus labentis et istam,

oro, si quis adhuc precibus locus, exue mentem.

320   Te propter Libycae gentes Nomadumque tyranni

odere, infensi Tyrii; te propter eundem

exstinctus pudor et, qua sola sidera adibam,

fama prior. Cui me moribundam deseris hospes

(hoc solum nomen quoniam de coniuge restat)?

325   Quid moror? An mea Pygmalion dum moenia frater

destruat aut captam ducat Gaetulus Iarbas?

Saltem si qua mihi de te suscepta fuisset

ante fugam suboles, si quis mihi parvulus aula

luderet Aeneas, qui te tamen ore referret,

330   non equidem omnino capta ac deserta viderer."

Dixerat. Ille Iovis monitis immota tenebat

lumina et obnixus curam sub corde premebat.

Tandem pauca refert: "Ego te, quae plurima fando

enumerare vales, numquam, regina, negabo

promeritam, nec me meminisse pigebit Elissae 335

dum memor ipse mei, dum spiritus hos regit artus.

Pro re pauca loquar. Neque ego hanc abscondere furto

speravi (ne finge) fugam, nec coniugis umquam

praetendi taedas aut haec in foedera veni.

Me si fata meis paterentur ducere vitam 340

auspiciis et sponte mea componere curas,

urbem Troianam primum dulcesque meorum

reliquias colerem, Priami tecta alta manerent,

et recidiva manu posuissem Pergama victis.

Sed nunc Italiam magnam Gryneus Apollo, 345

Italiam Lyciae iussere capessere sortes;

hic amor, haec patria est. si te Karthaginis arces

Phoenissam Libycaeque aspectus detinet urbis,

quae tandem Ausonia Teucros considere terra

invidia est? Et nos fas extera quaerere regna. 350

Me patris Anchisae, quotiens umentibus umbris

nox operit terras, quotiens astra ignea surgunt,

admonet in somnis et turbida terret imago;

me puer Ascanius capitisque iniuria cari,

quem regno Hesperiae fraudo et fatalibus arvis. 355

Nunc etiam interpres divum Iove missus ab ipso

(testor utrumque caput) celeres mandata per auras

detulit: ipse deum manifesto in lumine vidi

intrantem muros vocemque his auribus hausi.

360   Desine meque tuis incendere teque querelis;

Italiam non sponte sequor."

Talia dicentem iamdudum aversa tuetur

huc illuc volvens oculos totumque pererrat

luminibus tacitis et sic accensa profatur:

365   "Nec tibi diva parens generis nec Dardanus auctor,

perfide, sed duris genuit te cautibus horrens

Caucasus Hyrcanaeque admorunt ubera tigres.

Nam quid dissimulo aut quae me ad maiora reservo?

Num fletu ingemuit nostro? Num lumina flexit?

370   Num lacrimas victus dedit aut miseratus amantem est?

Quae quibus anteferam? Iam iam nec maxima Iuno

nec Saturnius haec oculis pater aspicit aequis.

Nusquam tuta fides. Eiectum litore, egentem

excepi et regni demens in parte locavi.

375   Amissam classem, socios a morte reduxi

(heu furiis incensa feror!): nunc augur Apollo,

nunc Lyciae sortes, nunc et Iove missus ab ipso

interpres divum fert horrida iussa per auras.

Scilicet is superis labor est, ea cura quietos

380   sollicitat. Neque te teneo neque dicta refello:

i, sequere Italiam ventis, pete regna per undas.

Spero equidem mediis, si quid pia numina possunt,

supplicia hausurum scopulis et nomine Dido

saepe vocaturum. Sequar atris ignibus absens

et, cum frigida mors anima seduxerit artus,   385

omnibus umbra locis adero. Dabis, improbe, poenas.

Audiam et haec Manes veniet mihi fama sub imos."

His medium dictis sermonem abrumpit et auras

aegra fugit seque ex oculis avertit et aufert,

linquens multa metu cunctantem et multa parantem   390

dicere. Suscipiunt famulae conlapsaque membra

marmoreo referunt thalamo stratisque reponunt.

At pius Aeneas, quamquam lenire dolentem

solando cupit et dictis avertere curas,

multa gemens magnoque animum labefactus amore   395

iussa tamen divum exsequitur classemque revisit.

Tum vero Teucri incumbunt et litore celsas

deducunt toto naves. Natat uncta carina,

frondentesque ferunt remos et robora silvis

infabricata fugae studio.   400

Migrantes cernas totaque ex urbe ruentes:

ac velut ingentem formicae farris acervum

cum populant hiemis memores tectoque reponunt,

it nigrum campis agmen praedamque per herbas

convectant calle angusto: pars grandia trudunt   405

obnixae frumenta umeris, pars agmina cogunt

castigantque moras, opere omnis semita fervet.

Quis tibi tum, Dido, cernenti talia sensus,

quosve dabas gemitus, cum litora fervere late

410   prospiceres arce ex summa, totumque videres

misceri ante oculos tantis clamoribus aequor!

Improbe Amor, quid non mortalia pectora cogis!

Ire iterum in lacrimas, iterum temptare precando

cogitur et supplex animos summittere amori,

415   ne quid inexpertum frustra moritura relinquat.

"Anna, vides toto properari litore circum:

undique convenere; vocat iam carbasus auras,

puppibus et laeti nautae imposuere coronas.

Hunc ego si potui tantum sperare dolorem,

420   et perferre, soror, potero. Miserae hoc tamen unum

exsequere, Anna, mihi; solam nam perfidus ille

te colere, arcanos etiam tibi credere sensus;

sola viri molles aditus et tempora noras.

I, soror, atque hostem supplex adfare superbum:

425   non ego cum Danais Troianam exscindere gentem

Aulide iuravi classemve ad Pergama misi,

nec patris Anchisae cinerem manesve revelli:

cur mea dicta negat duras demittere in aures?

Quo ruit? Extremum hoc miserae det munus amanti:

430   exspectet facilemque fugam ventosque ferentes.

Non iam coniugium antiquum, quod prodidit, oro,

nec pulchro ut Latio careat regnumque relinquat:

tempus inane peto, requiem spatiumque furori,

dum mea me victam doceat fortuna dolere.

Extremam hanc oro veniam (miserere sororis),   435

quam mihi cum dederit cumulatam morte remittam."

Talibus orabat, talesque miserrima fletus

fertque refertque soror. Sed nullis ille movetur

fletibus aut voces ullas tractabilis audit;

fata obstant placidasque viri deus obstruit aures.   440

Ac velut annoso validam cum robore quercum

Alpini Boreae nunc hinc nunc flatibus illinc

eruere inter se certant; it stridor, et altae

consternunt terram concusso stipite frondes;

ipsa haeret scopulis et quantum vertice ad auras   445

aetherias, tantum radice in Tartara tendit:

haud secus adsiduis hinc atque hinc vocibus heros

tunditur, et magno persentit pectore curas;

mens immota manet, lacrimae volvuntur inanes.

BOOK 4.642–705

At trepida et coeptis immanibus effera Dido

sanguineam volvens aciem, maculisque trementes

interfusa genas et pallida morte futura,

645   interiora domus inrumpit limina et altos

conscendit furibunda rogos ensemque recludit

Dardanium, non hos quaesitum munus in usus.

Hic, postquam Iliacas vestes notumque cubile

conspexit, paulum lacrimis et mente morata

650   incubuitque toro dixitque novissima verba:

"Dulces exuviae, dum fata deusque sinebat,

accipite hanc animam meque his exsolvite curis.

Vixi et quem dederat cursum Fortuna peregi,

et nunc magna mei sub terras ibit imago.

655   Urbem praeclaram statui, mea moenia vidi,

ulta virum poenas inimico a fratre recepi,

felix, heu nimium felix, si litora tantum

numquam Dardaniae tetigissent nostra carinae."

Dixit, et os impressa toro "Moriemur inultae,

660   sed moriamur" ait. "Sic, sic iuvat ire sub umbras.

Hauriat hunc oculis ignem crudelis ab alto

Dardanus, et nostrae secum ferat omina mortis."

Dixerat, atque illam media inter talia ferro

conlapsam aspiciunt comites, ensemque cruore

spumantem sparsasque manus. It clamor ad alta   665

atria: concussam bacchatur Fama per urbem.

Lamentis gemituque et femineo ululatu

tecta fremunt, resonat magnis plangoribus aether,

non aliter quam si immissis ruat hostibus omnis

Karthago aut antiqua Tyros, flammaeque furentes   670

culmina perque hominum volvantur perque deorum.

Audiit exanimis trepidoque exterrita cursu

unguibus ora soror foedans et pectora pugnis

per medios ruit, ac morientem nomine clamat:

"Hoc illud, germana, fuit? Me fraude petebas?   675

Hoc rogus iste mihi, hoc ignes araeque parabant?

Quid primum deserta querar? Comitemne sororem

sprevisti moriens? Eadem me ad fata vocasses:

idem ambas ferro dolor atque eadem hora tulisset.

His etiam struxi manibus patriosque vocavi   680

voce deos, sic te ut posita, crudelis, abessem?

Exstinxti te meque, soror, populumque patresque

Sidonios urbemque tuam. Date, vulnera lymphis

abluam et, extremus si quis super halitus errat,

ore legam." Sic fata gradus evaserat altos,   685

semianimemque sinu germanam amplexa fovebat

cum gemitu atque atros siccabat veste cruores.

Illa graves oculos conata attollere rursus

deficit; infixum stridit sub pectore vulnus.

690　Ter sese attollens cubitoque adnixa levavit,

ter revoluta toro est oculisque errantibus alto

quaesivit caelo lucem ingemuitque reperta.

Tum Iuno omnipotens longum miserata dolorem

difficilesque obitus Irim demisit Olympo

695　quae luctantem animam nexosque resolveret artus.

Nam quia nec fato merita nec morte peribat,

sed misera ante diem subitoque accensa furore,

nondum illi flavum Proserpina vertice crinem

abstulerat Stygioque caput damnaverat Orco.

700　Ergo Iris croceis per caelum roscida pennis

mille trahens varios adverso sole colores

devolat et supra caput astitit. "Hunc ego Diti

sacrum iussa fero teque isto corpore solvo":

Sic ait et dextra crinem secat, omnis et una

705　dilapsus calor atque in ventos vita recessit.

Sic fatur lacrimans, classique immittit habenas

et tandem Euboicis Cumarum adlabitur oris.

Obvertunt pelago proras; tum dente tenaci

ancora fundabat naves et litora curvae

praetexunt puppes. Iuvenum manus emicat ardens   5

litus in Hesperium; quaerit pars semina flammae

abstrusa in venis silicis, pars densa ferarum

tecta rapit silvas inventaque flumina monstrat.

At pius Aeneas arces quibus altus Apollo

praesidet horrendaeque procul secreta Sibyllae,   10

antrum immane, petit, magnam cui mentem animumque

Delius inspirat vates aperitque futura.

Iam subeunt Triviae lucos atque aurea tecta.

Daedalus, ut fama est, fugiens Minoia regna

praepetibus pennis ausus se credere caelo   15

insuetum per iter gelidas enavit ad Arctos,

Chalcidicaque levis tandem super astitit arce.

Redditus his primum terris tibi, Phoebe, sacravit

remigium alarum posuitque immania templa.

In foribus letum Androgeo; tum pendere poenas   20

Cecropidae iussi (miserum!) septena quotannis

corpora natorum; stat ductis sortibus urna.

Contra elata mari respondet Cnosia tellus:

hic crudelis amor tauri suppostaque furto

25   Pasiphae mixtumque genus prolesque biformis

Minotaurus inest, Veneris monimenta nefandae,

hic labor ille domus et inextricabilis error;

magnum reginae sed enim miseratus amorem

Daedalus ipse dolos tecti ambagesque resolvit,

30   caeca regens filo vestigia. Tu quoque magnam

partem opere in tanto, sineret dolor, Icare, haberes.

Bis conatus erat casus effingere in auro,

bis patriae cecidere manus. Quin protinus omnia

perlegerent oculis, ni iam praemissus Achates

35   adforet atque una Phoebi Triviaeque sacerdos,

Deiphobe Glauci, fatur quae talia regi:

"Non hoc ista sibi tempus spectacula poscit;

nunc grege de intacto septem mactare iuvencos

praestiterit, totidem lectas ex more bidentes."

40   Talibus adfata Aenean (nec sacra morantur

iussa viri) Teucros vocat alta in templa sacerdos.

Excisum Euboicae latus ingens rupis in antrum,

quo lati ducunt aditus centum, ostia centum,

unde ruunt totidem voces, responsa Sibyllae.

45   Ventum erat ad limen, cum virgo "Poscere fata

tempus" ait; "deus ecce deus!" Cui talia fanti

ante fores subito non vultus, non color unus,

non comptae mansere comae; sed pectus anhelum,

et rabie fera corda tument, maiorque videri

nec mortale sonans, adflata est numine quando   50

iam propiore dei. "Cessas in vota precesque,

Tros" ait "Aenea? Cessas? Neque enim ante dehiscent

attonitae magna ora domus." Et talia fata

conticuit. Gelidus Teucris per dura cucurrit

ossa tremor, funditque preces rex pectore ab imo: 55

"Phoebe, graves Troiae semper miserate labores,

Dardana qui Paridis derexti tela manusque

corpus in Aeacidae, magnas obeuntia terras

tot maria intravi duce te penitusque repostas

Massylum gentes praetentaque Syrtibus arva: 60

iam tandem Italiae fugientis prendimus oras.

Hac Troiana tenus fuerit fortuna secuta;

vos quoque Pergameae iam fas est parcere genti,

dique deaeque omnes, quibus obstitit Ilium et ingens

gloria Dardaniae. Tuque, o sanctissima vates,   65

praescia venturi, da (non indebita posco

regna meis fatis) Latio considere Teucros

errantesque deos agitataque numina Troiae.

Tum Phoebo et Triviae solido de marmore templum

instituam festosque dies de nomine Phoebi.   70

Te quoque magna manent regnis penetralia nostris:

hic ego namque tuas sortes arcanaque fata

dicta meae genti ponam, lectosque sacrabo,

alma, viros. Foliis tantum ne carmina manda,

75 ne turbata volent rapidis ludibria ventis;

ipsa canas oro." Finem dedit ore loquendi.

At Phoebi nondum patiens immanis in antro

bacchatur vates, magnum si pectore possit

excussisse deum; tanto magis ille fatigat

80 os rabidum, fera corda domans, fingitque premendo.

Ostia iamque domus patuere ingentia centum

sponte sua vatisque ferunt responsa per auras:

"O tandem magnis pelagi defuncte periclis

(sed terrae graviora manent), in regna Lavini

85 Dardanidae venient (mitte hanc de pectore curam),

sed non et venisse volent. Bella, horrida bella,

et Thybrim multo spumantem sanguine cerno.

Non Simois tibi nec Xanthus nec Dorica castra

defuerint; alius Latio iam partus Achilles,

90 natus et ipse dea; nec Teucris addita Iuno

usquam aberit, cum tu supplex in rebus egenis

quas gentes Italum aut quas non oraveris urbes!

Causa mali tanti coniunx iterum hospita Teucris

externique iterum thalami.

Tu ne cede malis, sed contra audentior ito, 95
qua tua te Fortuna sinet. Via prima salutis
(quod minime reris) Graia pandetur ab urbe."
Talibus ex adyto dictis Cumaea Sibylla
horrendas canit ambages antroque remugit,
obscuris vera involvens: ea frena furenti 100
concutit et stimulos sub pectore vertit Apollo.
Ut primum cessit furor et rabida ora quierunt,
incipit Aeneas heros: "Non ulla laborum,
o virgo, nova mi facies inopinave surgit;
omnia praecepi atque animo mecum ante peregi. 105
Unum oro: quando hic inferni ianua regis
dicitur et tenebrosa palus Acheronte refuso,
ire ad conspectum cari genitoris et ora
contingat; doceas iter et sacra ostia pandas.
Illum ego per flammas et mille sequentia tela 110
eripui his umeris medioque ex hoste recepi;
ille meum comitatus iter maria omnia mecum
atque omnes pelagique minas caelique ferebat,
invalidus, vires ultra sortemque senectae.
Quin, ut te supplex peterem et tua limina adirem, 115
idem orans mandata dabat. Gnatique patrisque,
alma, precor, miserere (potes namque omnia, nec te
nequiquam lucis Hecate praefecit Avernis),

si potuit manes accersere coniugis Orpheus

120 Threicia fretus cithara fidibusque canoris,

si fratrem Pollux alterna morte redemit

itque reditque viam totiens. Quid Thesea, magnum

quid memorem Alciden? Et mi genus ab Iove summo."

Talibus orabat dictis arasque tenebat,

125 cum sic orsa loqui vates: "Sate sanguine divum,

Tros Anchisiade, facilis descensus Averno:

noctes atque dies patet atri ianua Ditis;

sed revocare gradum superasque evadere ad auras,

hoc opus, hic labor est. Pauci, quos aequus amavit

130 Iuppiter aut ardens evexit ad aethera virtus,

dis geniti potuere. Tenent media omnia silvae,

Cocytusque sinu labens circumvenit atro.

Quod si tantus amor menti, si tanta cupido est,

bis Stygios innare lacus, bis nigra videre

135 Tartara, et insano iuvat indulgere labori,

accipe quae peragenda prius. Latet arbore opaca

aureus et foliis et lento vimine ramus,

Iunoni infernae dictus sacer; hunc tegit omnis

lucus et obscuris claudunt convallibus umbrae.

140 Sed non ante datur telluris operta subire

auricomos quam quis decerpserit arbore fetus.

Hoc sibi pulchra suum ferri Proserpina munus

instituit. Primo avulso non deficit alter

aureus, et simili frondescit virga metallo.

Ergo alte vestiga oculis et rite repertum 145

carpe manu; namque ipse volens facilisque sequetur,

si te fata vocant; aliter non viribus ullis

vincere, nec duro poteris convellere ferro.

Praeterea iacet exanimum tibi corpus amici

(heu nescis) totamque incestat funere classem, 150

dum consulta petis nostroque in limine pendes.

Sedibus hunc refer ante suis et conde sepulcro.

Duc nigras pecudes; ea prima piacula sunto.

Sic demum lucos Stygis et regna invia vivis

aspicies." Dixit, pressoque obmutuit ore. 155

Aeneas maesto defixus lumina vultu

ingreditur linquens antrum, caecosque volutat

eventus animo secum. Cui fidus Achates

it comes et paribus curis vestigia figit.

Multa inter sese vario sermone serebant, 160

quem socium exanimum vates, quod corpus humandum

diceret. Atque illi Misenum in litore sicco,

ut venere, vident indigna morte peremptum,

Misenum Aeoliden, quo non praestantior alter

aere ciere viros Martemque accendere cantu. 165

Hectoris hic magni fuerat comes, Hectora circum

et lituo pugnas insignis obibat et hasta.

Postquam illum vita victor spoliavit Achilles,

Dardanio Aeneae sese fortissimus heros

170 addiderat socium, non inferiora secutus.

Sed tum, forte cava dum personat aequora concha,

demens, et cantu vocat in certamina divos,

aemulus exceptum Triton, si credere dignum est,

inter saxa virum spumosa inmerserat unda.

175 Ergo omnes magno circum clamore fremebant,

praecipue pius Aeneas. Tum iussa Sibyllae,

haud mora, festinant flentes, aramque sepulcri

congerere arboribus caeloque educere certant.

Itur in antiquam silvam, stabula alta ferarum;

180 procumbunt piceae, sonat icta securibus ilex

fraxineaeque trabes cuneis et fissile robur

scinditur, advolvunt ingentes montibus ornos.

Nec non Aeneas opera inter talia primus

hortatur socios paribusque accingitur armis.

185 Atque haec ipse suo tristi cum corde volutat

aspectans silvam immensam, et sic forte precatur:

"Si nunc se nobis ille aureus arbore ramus

ostendat nemore in tanto! Quando omnia vere

heu nimium de te vates, Misene, locuta est."

190 Vix ea fatus erat, geminae cum forte columbae

ipsa sub ora viri caelo venere volantes,

et viridi sedere solo. Tum maximus heros

maternas agnoscit aves laetusque precatur:

"Este duces, o, si qua via est, cursumque per auras

derigite in lucos ubi pinguem dives opacat 195

ramus humum. Tuque, o, dubiis ne defice rebus,

diva parens." Sic effatus vestigia pressit

observans quae signa ferant, quo tendere pergant.

Pascentes illae tantum prodire volando

quantum acie possent oculi servare sequentum. 200

Inde ubi venere ad fauces grave olentis Averni,

tollunt se celeres liquidumque per aera lapsae

sedibus optatis gemina super arbore sidunt,

discolor unde auri per ramos aura refulsit.

Quale solet silvis brumali frigore viscum 205

fronde virere nova, quod non sua seminat arbos,

et croceo fetu teretes circumdare truncos,

talis erat species auri frondentis opaca

ilice, sic leni crepitabat brattea vento.

Corripit Aeneas extemplo avidusque refringit 210

cunctantem, et vatis portat sub tecta Sibyllae.

450   Inter quas Phoenissa recens a vulnere Dido

errabat silva in magna; quam Troius heros

ut primum iuxta stetit agnovitque per umbras

obscuram, qualem primo qui surgere mense

aut videt aut vidisse putat per nubila lunam,

455   demisit lacrimas dulcique adfatus amore est:

"Infelix Dido, verus mihi nuntius ergo

venerat exstinctam ferroque extrema secutam?

Funeris heu tibi causa fui? Per sidera iuro,

per superos et si qua fides tellure sub ima est,

460   invitus, regina, tuo de litore cessi.

Sed me iussa deum, quae nunc has ire per umbras,

per loca senta situ cogunt noctemque profundam,

imperiis egere suis; nec credere quivi

hunc tantum tibi me discessu ferre dolorem.

465   Siste gradum teque aspectu ne subtrahe nostro.

Quem fugis? Extremum fato quod te adloquor hoc est."

Talibus Aeneas ardentem et torva tuentem

lenibat dictis animum lacrimasque ciebat.

Illa solo fixos oculos aversa tenebat

470   nec magis incepto vultum sermone movetur

quam si dura silex aut stet Marpesia cautes.

Tandem corripuit sese atque inimica refugit

in nemus umbriferum, coniunx ubi pristinus illi

respondet curis aequatque Sychaeus amorem.

Nec minus Aeneas casu concussus iniquo 475

prosequitur lacrimis longe et miseratur euntem.

"Excudent alii spirantia mollius aera

(credo equidem), vivos ducent de marmore vultus,

orabunt causas melius, caelique meatus

850   describent radio et surgentia sidera dicent:

tu regere imperio populos, Romane, memento

(hae tibi erunt artes), pacique imponere morem,

parcere subiectis et debellare superbos."

Sic pater Anchises, atque haec mirantibus addit:

855   "Aspice, ut insignis spoliis Marcellus opimis

ingreditur victorque viros supereminet omnes.

Hic rem Romanam magno turbante tumultu

sistet eques, sternet Poenos Gallumque rebellem,

tertiaque arma patri suspendet capta Quirino."

860   Atque hic Aeneas (una namque ire videbat

egregium forma iuvenem et fulgentibus armis,

sed frons laeta parum et deiecto lumina vultu)

"Quis, pater, ille, virum qui sic comitatur euntem?

Filius, anne aliquis magna de stirpe nepotum?

865   Qui strepitus circa comitum! Quantum instar in ipso!

Sed nox atra caput tristi circumvolat umbra."

Tum pater Anchises lacrimis ingressus obortis:

"O gnate, ingentem luctum ne quaere tuorum;

ostendent terris hunc tantum fata neque ultra
esse sinent. Nimium vobis Romana propago   870
visa potens, superi, propria haec si dona fuissent.
Quantos ille virum magnam Mavortis ad urbem
campus aget gemitus! Vel quae, Tiberine, videbis
funera, cum tumulum praeterlabere recentem!
Nec puer Iliaca quisquam de gente Latinos   875
in tantum spe tollet avos, nec Romula quondam
ullo se tantum tellus iactabit alumno.
Heu pietas, heu prisca fides invictaque bello
dextera! Non illi se quisquam impune tulisset
obvius armato, seu cum pedes iret in hostem   880
seu spumantis equi foderet calcaribus armos.
Heu, miserande puer, si qua fata aspera rumpas—
tu Marcellus eris. Manibus date lilia plenis
purpureos spargam flores animamque nepotis
his saltem accumulem donis, et fungar inani   885
munere." Sic tota passim regione vagantur
aeris in campis latis atque omnia lustrant.
Quae postquam Anchises natum per singula duxit
incenditque animum famae venientis amore,
exim bella viro memorat quae deinde gerenda,   890
Laurentesque docet populos urbemque Latini,
et quo quemque modo fugiatque feratque laborem.

Sunt geminae Somni portae, quarum altera fertur

cornea, qua veris facilis datur exitus umbris,

895   altera candenti perfecta nitens elephanto,

sed falsa ad caelum mittunt insomnia Manes.

His ibi tum natum Anchises unaque Sibyllam

prosequitur dictis portaque emittit eburna;

ille viam secat ad naves sociosque revisit.

900   Tum se ad Caietae recto fert limite portum.

Ancora de prora iacitur; stant litore puppes.

Quem sic Pallas petit ante precatus: 420

"Da nunc, Thybri pater, ferro, quod missile libro,

fortunam atque viam duri per pectus Halaesi.

Haec arma exuviasque viri tua quercus habebit."

Audiit illa deus; dum texit Imaona Halaesus,

Arcadio infelix telo dat pectus inermum.   425

At non caede viri tanta perterrita Lausus,

pars ingens belli, sinit agmina: primus Abantem

oppositum interimit, pugnae nodumque moramque.

Sternitur Arcadiae proles, sternuntur Etrusci

et vos, O Grais imperdita corpora, Teucri.   430

Agmina concurrunt ducibusque et viribus aequis;

extremi addensent acies nec turba moveri

tela manusque sinit. Hinc Pallas instat et urget,

hinc contra Lausus, nec multum discrepat aetas,

egregii forma, sed quis Fortuna negarat   435

in patriam reditus. Ipsos concurrere passus

haud tamen inter se magni regnator Olympi;

mox illos sua fata manent maiore sub hoste.

Interea soror alma monet succedere Lauso

Turnum, qui volucri curru medium secat agmen.   440

Ut vidit socios: "Tempus desistere pugnae;

solus ego in Pallanta feror, soli mihi Pallas

debetur; cuperem ipse parens spectator adesset."

Haec ait, et socii cesserunt aequore iusso.

445 At Rutulum abscessu iuvenis tum iussa superba

miratus stupet in Turno corpusque per ingens

lumina volvit obitque truci procul omnia visu,

talibus et dictis it contra dicta tyranni:

"Aut spoliis ego iam raptis laudabor opimis

450 aut leto insigni: sorti pater aequus utrique est.

Tolle minas." Fatus medium procedit in aequor;

frigidus Arcadibus coit in praecordia sanguis.

Desiluit Turnus biiugis, pedes apparat ire

comminus; utque leo, specula cum vidit ab alta

455 stare procul campis meditantem in proelia taurum,

advolat, haud alia est Turni venientis imago.

Hunc ubi contiguum missae fore credidit hastae,

ire prior Pallas, si qua fors adiuvet ausum

viribus imparibus, magnumque ita ad aethera fatur:

460 "Per patris hospitium et mensas, quas advena adisti,

te precor, Alcide, coeptis ingentibus adsis.

Cernat semineci sibi me rapere arma cruenta

victoremque ferant morientia lumina Turni."

Audiit Alcides iuvenem magnumque sub imo

465 corde premit gemitum lacrimasque effundit inanes.

Tum genitor natum dictis adfatur amicis:

"Stat sua cuique dies, breve et inreparabile tempus

omnibus est vitae; sed famam extendere factis,

hoc virtutis opus. Troiae sub moenibus altis

tot gnati cecidere deum, quin occidit una　　　　　470

Sarpedon, mea progenies; etiam sua Turnum

fata vocant metasque dati pervenit ad aevi."

Sic ait, atque oculos Rutulorum reicit arvis.

At Pallas magnis emittit viribus hastam

vaginaque cava fulgentem deripit ensem.　　　　　475

Illa volans umeri surgunt qua tegmina summa

incidit, atque viam clipei molita per oras

tandem etiam magno strinxit de corpore Turni.

Hic Turnus ferro praefixum robur acuto

in Pallanta diu librans iacit atque ita fatur:　　　480

"Aspice num mage sit nostrum penetrabile telum."

Dixerat; at clipeum, tot ferri terga, tot aeris,

quem pellis totiens obeat circumdata tauri,

vibranti cuspis medium transverberat ictu

loricaeque moras et pectus perforat ingens.　　　485

Ille rapit calidum frustra de vulnere telum:

una eademque via sanguis animusque sequuntur.

Corruit in vulnus (sonitum super arma dedere)

et terram hostilem moriens petit ore cruento.

490   Quem Turnus super adsistens:

"Arcades, haec" inquit "memores mea dicta referte

Evandro: qualem meruit, Pallanta remitto.

Quisquis honos tumuli, quidquid solamen humandi est,

largior. Haud illi stabunt Aeneia parvo

495   hospitia." Et laevo pressit pede talia fatus

exanimem rapiens immania pondera baltei

impressumque nefas: una sub nocte iugali

caesa manus iuvenum foede thalamique cruenti,

quae Clonus Eurytides multo caelaverat auro;

500   quo nunc Turnus ovat spolio gaudetque potitus.

Nescia mens hominum fati sortisque futurae

et servare modum rebus sublata secundis!

Turno tempus erit magno cum optaverit emptum

intactum Pallanta, et cum spolia ista diemque

505   oderit. At socii multo gemitu lacrimisque

impositum scuto referunt Pallanta frequentes.

O dolor atque decus magnum rediture parenti,

haec te prima dies bello dedit, haec eadem aufert,

cum tamen ingentes Rutulorum linquis acervos!

Iunonem interea rex omnipotentis Olympi

adloquitur fulva pugnas de nube tuentem:

"Quae iam finis erit, coniunx? Quid denique restat?

Indigetem Aenean scis ipsa et scire fateris

deberi caelo fatisque ad sidera tolli.   795

Quid struis? Aut qua spe gelidis in nubibus haeres?

Mortalin decuit violari vulnere divum?

Aut ensem (quid enim sine te Iuturna valeret?)

ereptum reddi Turno et vim crescere victis?

Desine iam tandem precibusque inflectere nostris,   800

ne te tantus edit tacitam dolor et mihi curae

saepe tuo dulci tristes ex ore recursent.

Ventum ad supremum est. Terris agitare vel undis

Troianos potuisti, infandum accendere bellum,

deformare domum et luctu miscere hymenaeos: 805

ulterius temptare veto." Sic Iuppiter orsus;

sic dea summisso contra Saturnia vultu:

"Ista quidem quia nota mihi tua, magne, voluntas,

Iuppiter, et Turnum et terras invita reliqui;

nec tu me aeria solam nunc sede videres   810

digna indigna pati, sed flammis cincta sub ipsa

starem acie traheremque inimica in proelia Teucros.

Iuturnam misero (fateor) succurrere fratri

suasi et pro vita maiora audere probavi,

815 non ut tela tamen, non ut contenderet arcum;

adiuro Stygii caput implacabile fontis,

una superstitio superis quae reddita divis.

Et nunc cedo equidem pugnasque exosa relinquo.

Illud te, nulla fati quod lege tenetur,

820 pro Latio obtestor, pro maiestate tuorum:

cum iam conubiis pacem felicibus (esto)

component, cum iam leges et foedera iungent,

ne vetus indigenas nomen mutare Latinos

neu Troas fieri iubeas Teucrosque vocari

825 aut vocem mutare viros aut vertere vestem.

Sit Latium, sint Albani per saecula reges,

sit Romana potens Itala virtute propago:

occidit, occideritque sinas cum nomine Troia."

Olli subridens hominum rerumque repertor:

830 "Es germana Iovis Saturnique altera proles,

irarum tantos volvis sub pectore fluctus.

Verum age et inceptum frustra summitte furorem:

do quod vis, et me victusque volensque remitto.

Sermonem Ausonii patrium moresque tenebunt,

835 utque est nomen erit; commixti corpore tantum

subsident Teucri. Morem ritusque sacrorum

adiciam faciamque omnes uno ore Latinos.

Hinc genus Ausonio mixtum quod sanguine surget,

supra homines, supra ire deos pietate videbis,

nec gens ulla tuos aeque celebrabit honores." 840

Adnuit his Iuno et mentem laetata retorsit;

interea excedit caelo nubemque relinquit.

BOOK 12.887–952

Aeneas instat contra telumque coruscat

ingens arboreum, et saevo sic pectore fatur:

"Quae nunc deinde mora est? Aut quid iam, Turne, retractas?

890   Non cursu, saevis certandum est comminus armis.

Verte omnes tete in facies et contrahe quidquid

sive animis sive arte vales; opta ardua pennis

astra sequi clausumque cava te condere terra."

Ille caput quassans: "Non me tua fervida terrent

895   dicta, ferox; di me terrent et Iuppiter hostis."

Nec plura effatus saxum circumspicit ingens,

saxum antiquum ingens, campo quod forte iacebat,

limes agro positus litem ut discerneret arvis.

Vix illum lecti bis sex cervice subirent,

900   qualia nunc hominum producit corpora tellus;

ille manu raptum trepida torquebat in hostem

altior insurgens et cursu concitus heros.

Sed neque currentem se nec cognoscit euntem

tollentemve manu saxumve immane moventem;

905   genua labant, gelidus concrevit frigore sanguis.

Tum lapis ipse viri vacuum per inane volutus

nec spatium evasit totum neque pertulit ictum.

Ac velut in somnis, oculos ubi languida pressit

nocte quies, nequiquam avidos extendere cursus

velle videmur et in mediis conatibus aegri   910

succidimus; non lingua valet, non corpore notae

sufficiunt vires nec vox aut verba sequuntur:

sic Turno, quacumque viam virtute petivit,

successum dea dira negat. Tum pectore sensus

vertuntur varii; Rutulos aspectat et urbem   915

cunctaturque metu letumque instare tremescit,

nec quo se eripiat, nec qua vi tendat in hostem,

nec currus usquam videt aurigamve sororem.

Cunctanti telum Aeneas fatale coruscat,

sortitus fortunam oculis, et corpore toto   920

eminus intorquet. Murali concita numquam

tormento sic saxa fremunt nec fulmine tanti

dissultant crepitus. Volat atri turbinis instar

exitium dirum hasta ferens orasque recludit

loricae et clipei extremos septemplicis orbes;   925

per medium stridens transit femur. Incidit ictus

ingens ad terram duplicato poplite Turnus.

Consurgunt gemitu Rutuli totusque remugit

mons circum et vocem late nemora alta remittunt.

Ille humilis supplex oculos dextramque precantem   930

protendens "Equidem merui nec deprecor" inquit:

"utere sorte tua. Miseri te si qua parentis

tangere cura potest, oro (fuit et tibi talis

Anchises genitor) Dauni miserere senectae

935 et me, seu corpus spoliatum lumine mavis,

redde meis. Vicisti et victum tendere palmas

Ausonii videre; tua est Lavinia coniunx,

ulterius ne tende odiis." Stetit acer in armis

Aeneas volvens oculos dextramque repressit;

940 et iam iamque magis cunctantem flectere sermo

coeperat, infelix umero cum apparuit alto

balteus et notis fulserunt cingula bullis

Pallantis pueri, victum quem vulnere Turnus

straverat atque umeris inimicum insigne gerebat.

945 Ille, oculis postquam saevi monimenta doloris

exuviasque hausit, furiis accensus et ira

terribilis: "Tune hinc spoliis indute meorum

eripiare mihi? Pallas te hoc vulnere, Pallas

immolat et poenam scelerato ex sanguine sumit."

950 Hoc dicens ferrum adverso sub pectore condit

fervidus; ast illi solvuntur frigore membra

vitaque cum gemitu fugit indignata sub umbras.

VERGIL ANCILLARY MATERIALS

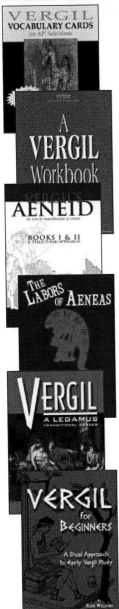

VERGIL VOCABULARY CARDS for AP* Selections
Dennis De Young

587 vocabulary cards divided by frequency of occurrence, grammatical form summaries reference sheets (*Graphic Latin Grammar*), reference sheets on Meter; Rhetorical Terms, Figures of Speech, and Rhetorical Devices.

184 pp. (2005) Paperback, ISBN 978-0-86516-610-3

A VERGIL WORKBOOK
Katherine Bradley and Barbara Weiden Boyd

AP* Latin text with exercises to give practice in content, translation, meter, grammar, syntax, vocabulary, figures of speech, and literary analysis. Can be used with all Vergil AP* textbooks.

Student Text: xiv + 261 pp. (2006) Paperback, ISBN 978-0-86516-614-1
Teacher's Manual: (Forthcoming) Paperback, ISBN 978-0-86516-651-6

VERGIL'S AENEID, BOOKS I & II
A Structural Approach
Waldo E. Sweet

Latin text with paraphrase on facing pages. Commentary in Latin from Servius and others.

163 pp. (1960, Reprint 1983) Paperback, ISBN 978-0-86516-023-1

THE LABORS OF AENEAS:
What A Pain It Was to Found the Roman Race
Rose Williams

A delightful retelling of Vergil's entire *Aeneid* that is faithful to the story's facts, but told in a witty, droll fashion.

vi + 108 pp. (2003) Paperback, ISBN 978-0-86516-556-4

VERGIL: A LEGAMUS Transitional Reader
Thomas J. Sienkewicz and LeaAnn A. Osburn

11 selections (about 200 lines) from *Aeneid* I, II, and IV, designed as a bridge between elementary and intermediate Latin. Many reading aids, introductory materials, illustrations, and a grammatical appendix.

xxiv + 136 pp. (2004) Paperback, ISBN 978-0-86516-578-6

VERGIL FOR BEGINNERS
A Dual Approach to Early Vergil Study
Rose Williams

For first-year high school or second-semester college Latin students, this ancillary text presents six short selections from Vergil's *Aeneid*, each accompanied by grammar exercises and vocabulary aids. Exercises present and review key elements of grammar for each reading selection, and Latin synonyms promote reading comprehension for students just beginning to read Vergil.

Student Text: x + 86 pp. (2006) Paperback, ISBN 978-0-86516-628-8
Teacher's Guide: (forthcoming), ISBN 978-0-86516-629-5

BOLCHAZY-CARDUCCI PUBLISHERS, INC.
www.BOLCHAZY.com

VERGIL MATERIALS TO ENRICH COMPREHENSION

VERGIL'S *AENEID:* Hero, War, Humanity
G. B. Cobbold

A novelized English version of the entire *Aeneid*, with engaging and helpful reader aids.

xviii + 366 pp. (2005) Paperback, ISBN 978-0-86516-596-0

POET & ARTIST: Imaging the *Aeneid*
Henry V. Bender and David Califf

Book/CD combination that juxtaposes images with the AP* text of Vergil and thought-provoking questions. Encourages students to examine the text more closely and reflect critically upon it.

xvi + 88 pp. (2004) Paperback + CD-ROM, ISBN 978-0-86516-585-4

THE ART OF THE AENEID, 2nd edition
William S. Anderson

"A useful start on Rome's finest poem," according to the author, William S. Anderson. Background on Vergil and the genre of epic, followed by analysis of each of the twelve books in turn.

vi + 138 pp. (2005, 2nd ed., 1989 reprint of 1969 ed.)
Paperback, ISBN 978-0-86516-598-4

WHY VERGIL? A Collection of Interpretations
Stephanie Quinn, ed.

43 selections by 38 authors, with Quinn's powerful, extensive Introduction and Conclusion.

xxi + 451 pp. (2000); Paperback, ISBN 978-0-86516-418-5
Hardbound, ISBN 978-0-86516-435-2

PARSED VERGIL:
Completely Scanned-Parsed Vergil's *Aeneid* Book I
With Interlinear and Marginal Translations
Archibald A. Maclardy

Maclardy's volume is an irreplaceable primary resource. At the bottom of each page below the text, each Latin word is completely parsed, with helpful references to standard grammars, discussions of word derivations, and notations on word frequencies. The Latin text is completely scanned and accompanied by an interlinear word-for-word translation, with a more polished translation in the margins.

iv + 348 pp. (2005, Reprint of 1899, 1901 edtion) Paperback, ISBN 978-0-86516-630-1

VERGIL'S AENEID 8 & 11:
Italy & Rome
Barbara Weiden Boyd

Latin text of 395 lines of the *Aeneid*: 608–673 (Shield of Aeneas), 11.498–596 (Introduction of Camilla), and 11.664–835 (Camilla's heroism and defeat), with same-page vocabulary and notes.

x + 96 pp. (2006) Paperback, ISBN 978-0-86516-580-9

*AP is a registered trademark of the College Entrance Examination Board, which was not involved in the production of, and does not endorse, this product.

BOLCHAZY-CARDUCCI PUBLISHERS, INC.
WWW.BOLCHAZY.COM